Beyond the Pond

The Untold Story of Marble Brook Elementary School

James Randall

D1279713

Foreword

I am married to a teacher who experienced the Sandy Hook Elementary School tragedy. Since that time, I have observed how this trauma has impacted my spouse, her co-workers, parents, children, and the community. Now, over ten years later, many lives are still held hostage by that unthinkable reality.

The local community has built a beautiful flowing water memorial to those lives that were lost that day. No doubt those precious lives should be remembered. Yet to let that one event erase the school's identity and rob us of many special memories for which we can give thanks is another form of loss.

The purpose of this book is to memorialize through historical fiction the Sandy Hook school from both the animal and human perspectives as Nature and people were connected there. Human consciousness is too often unaware of the full impact of any given act, kindness, or loss in the natural world. As in any relationship, when we get to know others, we realize that we share many of the same challenges, and our respect for and behaviors toward each other change.

In the end, my prayer is that *Beyond the Pond* will produce good thoughts that refresh and enable our hearts to sing and our minds to be renewed, spurring us to seek understanding and new relationships that protect life in all forms in the world around us.

Author, James Randall

This book is dedicated to my wife Robin and all those who make schools a place that help young children, their families, and communities find fuller and more meaningful lives and relationships.

Keep me as the apple of the eye, hide me under the shadow of thy wings.
Psalm 17:8 KJV

Chapter 1
Ducks

Quack!! Qua-qua-a-ack!!!! Nails had appeared out of the spring sun's glare, her wings tucked to build maximum velocity, targeting Blossom's recently hatched flock of downy brown and yellow ducklings with her pin sharp talons. These were the six survivors of the original thirteen eggs Blossom had started to incubate. She had only taken one or two breaks a day, leaving the nest unguarded to forage for food, but it had still allowed the raccoons, crows, and a rat snake enough opportunities to eat over half of the eggs before they hatched.

The ducklings had responded instantly to Blossom's warning, diving in a blink to the bottom of their small estuary's pond. Nails' talons raked the water but were empty as the hawk's shadow moved quickly over the bottom of the pond.

Having escaped the raptor's sortie, there was still danger in the mossy depths from Chomps and Cuddles, the resident snapping turtles who were usually burrowed down into the soft sediment of the pond, waiting for a meal to stray too close. Fortunately, today they were at the other end of the pond, contemplating when

Chomps would travel up the embankment to find some soft sandy soil and mulch to deposit and bury her own clutch of rubbery eggs, leaving them to be incubated by the sun-warmed earth.

Blossom was relieved as each downy puff of peeping life popped back up, sending little circles across the water's surface. Two, then another one, two more, and finally, the last one broke onto the pond's sky-mirrored film. Seeking comfort, they paddled up close to her. Two still frantically peeping climbed up onto her back. From a distance, they now looked like one large duck, as the little single parent family stayed tightly bunched and moved into the cover of a fallen tree that the winter ice had overwhelmed, snapping its trunk, leaving it to rest on the water's edge.

The embarrassed Nails, who had been outmaneuvered by Blossom and her infant ducks, soared away, not wanting to expend the effort to make another attempt only to hear the trash talking peeps of the little waterfowl once again. Besides, why should she since they were only a snack and not a real meal like a chipmunk, vole, or baby rabbit, all of whom resided in the high meadow and surrounding woods? Her eyases (baby hawks) would not go hungry. Her mate Eyeballs was a good provider too and had been scooping up plenty of furry and feathered meals for their own two hatchlings.

As the afternoon shadows lengthened, the little duck family gradually relaxed. One duckling saw an army of tadpoles and was giving chase, although he was within one leap of their mother Legs, who along with other bullfrogs and tree frogs, was beginning to warm up her vocal cords for an evening of guttural croaking. There were hundreds of tadpoles, their little black bodies each with a tapered tail, wiggling in retreat into the submerged leaf litter along the pool's edge. He was determined to eat them, but his aim and timing were bad, so he missed almost every time.

Finally, the two ducklings on her back decided to rejoin their four siblings, and they slid into the water. Upon seeing a water spider, Drippy immediately decided to give chase. The spider, however, was quick, and it skated across the water's film, keeping well ahead of its paddling pursuer. The second one named Petals, on the other hand, was following her mother's example and filtering out duckweed using her beak plates.

The sun faded behind the hillside, and the duckling brood snuggled up to Blossom as the afternoon warmth yielded to the cool evening air. A wispy fog formed low across their still beaver pond. Legs and her relatives started filling the empty night with their croaks and peeps, which coupled with chirping insects made for a growing chorus of sentinels whose silence usually signaled the approach of an unwanted visitor, a storm, or other changes to their part of the world.

"Rest my little ones," Blossom whispered. "Rest." Her mate had left after she laid the first of the eggs, and the protection of the brood had been her sole responsibility since then. In truth, that was a good thing, as her mate's handsome green head with purplish hue, white neck ring, and bright white and gray body would have been a flashing billboard, saying, "Here is Blossom's nest!" Still, a little support would have been nice. Someone to watch the eggs when she needed to eat or to bring her a small fish, but alas that would attract even more hungry eyes to her and the nest. *Oh well,* she sighed. *I wish there was a nesting place free of predators where my eggs were safe before they hatched. The threats here never stop coming,* she mused, thinking about what challenges the night and coming day would bring.

Chapter 2
Job Assignments

Principal Peggy Booker set high goals for her teachers, staff, and students. With her leadership and advocacy, along with the staff's hard work, Marble Brook Elementary had been recognized as a Presidential Blue-Ribbon School—an achievement that she, along with the teachers, support staff, parents, students, and school board (oh, and not to forget, realtors) proudly shared with friends, colleagues, and families (as well as prospective home buyers) from other schools, towns, states, and countries.

Located in a historic and quintessential New England town, Marble Brook Elementary opened in the 1950s, serving students in kindergarten through grade six. When enrollment peaked at over 800, temporary classroom space was constructed behind the main building. A new intermediate school was established in 2002, absorbing the fifth and sixth graders which reduced Marble Brook's student population to under 500. This left the temporary buildings idle, except for one room being used for the storage of furniture and equipment.

Marble Brook's main building was a large, one-level square

with a center courtyard, accessible from the building through two different glass doors located on the south side of the building. The doors on the eastern end of that wall led straight through the school to an outside doorway, and the asphalted playground and recreation fields used for recesses and the town's after-school sports programs.

Most of the classrooms' entrances were in the central hallways, along with the library and support center. Wandering through the building was like being lost in the forest without a compass— eventually you would wind up where you started if you proceeded in one direction.

The north side hallway housed the cafeteria and gym. Opposite them, facing the courtyard, were the administration and nurse's offices, along with additional classrooms.

On this Monday morning in 2009, Mrs. Helen Dean had arrived earlier than usual to update the week's seventeen job assignments for her twenty-one second graders before the buses and parents dropped them off at eight-thirty a.m. Normally she did this on Friday afternoons after dismissal, but the previous week her youngest son had had a baseball game after school, and she hadn't wanted to miss seeing him play.

Based on her standard student rotation, this week Lucas would take the attendance report to the office; Callan would deliver the lunch order to the cafeteria; Lyra would be the paper manager, handing out worksheets; the black board cleaner would be Ryan; and the pledge leader would be Mia. "Oh remember, you need to send Mia's mom a note about the missing reading assessment," she said out loud to herself.

Mrs. Dean often spoke aloud when she was alone. One day when her students were in gym class, a passing parent's ear caught: "What a dummy you are. You did it again. Dummy!" "My, oh my," the parent thought. "A teacher should never talk to a child that way." In actuality, Mrs. Dean had just been reprimanding herself for forgetting to save a grading worksheet file she had just spent thirty minutes updating on her computer. Personal computers were only an idea being worked on in someone's garage when she was in college in the mid-nineteen seventies, and like others of her generation she was not very experienced with them.

Completing the week's job assignments, Rachel and Dylan would handle feeding the birds; Ryan would be line leader; the two substitutes for when the others were absent would-be Russell and Lena. The loudspeaker mounted above the chalkboard in the front of the room suddenly squawked.

Sitting on top of the speaker's wood housing was her coiled stuffed snake toy she had named Kaa after the slithering *Jungle Book* character. She thought of the hypnotic "Trust in me-e-e-e" and stare from the Disney movie. "Mrs. Dean, please come to the office. Mrs. Booker needs to speak to you." The speaker squawked again as school office manager and chief petty officer Betty of her majesty's ship Marble Brook clicked off the mic. Betty's responses could be short and at times hard, especially for new teachers that did not follow her rules. Truth be known, though, she was a very caring person, a certified softy, especially for students and families who were struggling with life.

"Oh my, what is it now?" Helen said quietly to herself. "I must remember to update the job assignments in my book later so I can show my budding lawyers some clear irrefutable evidence that they have not been unjustly deprived from being assigned their favorite jobs." Of course, the preferred tasks were ones that allowed the students to leave the classroom.

Off she headed to her captain's office. She understood being called before the mast, as her dad had graduated as president of his class from the U.S. Naval Academy in Annapolis. *I wonder what it will be about?* she thought to herself, exhaling, and taking a deep breath to calm her nerves. *Most likely some parent complaint.*

Chapter 3
Challenges

"Go on in," Betty smiled, glancing toward Principal Booker's doorway. Peggy Booker's office spoke to her strong sense of order and control. Her desk and shelves were filled, yet uncluttered, and everything had a place.

"Good morning, Helen," Peggy greeted her. "Thanks for coming down so quickly. I wanted to give you a heads-up that we are assigning a new student to your class. He is expected to report on Thursday. Since you have the students with allergies for your grade, I am forced to assign him to your room, even though I know it is already the largest second grade class at twenty-one. His name is Randy Jackson, and his parents are Ruth Ann and Brad. They moved here from San Marcos, California for Brad's work. They are a blended family, and Randy has two older siblings from his mom's first marriage. Both are in middle school."

California . . . my people Helen thought as she had been born at Camp Pendleton, one of many stops growing up in a military family.

"Randy is a special needs student," Peggy continued. "Per his mother, he is identified as autistic, which I have confirmed with the

California school. He will be assigned an Educational Assistant (EA). I have asked Susie to convene the special needs team to meet with you once we have his school records. We will have a desk and chair pulled out of storage tomorrow so you can decide how you want to position Randy in the classroom. Do you have any questions or concerns?" Peggy looked up from Randy's file folder that she had positioned on the left edge of her desk.

"Do you know who the EA will be?" Helen asked. "We are interviewing candidates this afternoon and hope to have a decision by Wednesday," the principal replied. "You know the process though, and the person may not be on board before Randy arrives. I will have Betty ensure we have one of the interns available to assist if that is the case. Anything else?" Peggy looked squarely at Helen with almost a smile.

"Not now. I need to get back to the classroom. The buses will be arriving soon," Helen said, noticing on the desk clock that it was almost eight-thirty. "Thanks for letting me know."

"Thank you, Helen. Randy is a lucky young man to have you," Peggy said, then returned to the complaint about a new kindergarten teacher who was struggling with a child's parents. The parents believed their five-year-old was exceptional and would require an accelerated lesson strategy to fit his genius. Obviously, Lake Tofargon was not the only place where all children were above the median.

Peggy Booker hired people for whom teaching was a calling, not just a job. She backed them up and helped them become better educators and was therefore proud to lead. The reality was that the little boy was not exceptional. She would need to assure his parents that he was receiving instruction that would allow him to reach his full potential. There was a constant learning curve to relate to and help students, parents, and teachers succeed together.

Hovering young parents were forgiven for their parental exuberance over their first child. Gently addressing the naïve demands and parental bias about their child could be painful, but it

8

was important. Done properly, it could also be a rewarding experience.

Parental pressure on some children to be in the top 1 percent often had the opposite effect by creating low self-esteem in some instances where they were not capable of the demanded level of performance but were still really good kids with strong potential. This was in stark contrast to parents she never saw when she was a young teacher in an inner-city school, where systemic economic and social realities left children to fend for themselves at an early age with little parental support at school.

Most new teachers generally did not have the experience and confidence to push back on unreasonable and inappropriate parental demands. Peggy's job was to provide support before a good teacher became so overwhelmed and discouraged that they quit the profession. And she did.

Exiting the principal's office, Helen saw students coming in the front entrance. "Hi, Mrs. Dean," said a waving, curly blonde-haired, third grade girl with a bright pink backpack, which looked to be half her size and had a multi-colored unicorn stuffed animal bouncing off the zipper tag. Rita had been in Helen's class last year, and she had a little brother Tim, who was now in Mrs. Rogers' first grade class. Her mom Cynthia had been a classroom parent. Cynthia's positive, helpful persona was reflected in both children.

"Are you enjoying being in Mrs. Broyles's class, Rita?" Helen asked. "Yes sir, reedy-dee-dee-dee, Mrs. Dean. See you later!" She chuckled her way down the hall. That moment of joy in motion briefly cleared Helen's mind of her concern on how Randy's unknown autistic behaviors would impact her class atmosphere, and if Randy would be accepted by his new classmates.

"Helen let's focus. You need to take care of today," she said to herself, resetting her thinking as she quickly moved to get to her classroom in time to greet her pupils.

Chapter 4
Growing Up

Things were always changing around the beaver pond estuary. A sandy south facing embankment had a hole recently excavated by Chomps, where she had deposited twenty-six ping-pong size leathery white eggs, then covered them over with sand and leaf litter before retreating to the water. If her nest was not disturbed and the summer temperatures were normal, she hoped to see the sand start erupting in early September with little snappers, assuming the racoons or skunks did not find the eggs first.

The snapper hatchlings would then be faced with threats from more predators, including blue herons, foxes, coyotes, even crows and other mature turtles. The beaver pond estuary was a tough neighborhood for young animals. Snapping turtles were especially vulnerable, as unlike other turtles, they could not pull their bodies back into their shell, so retreating inwards was not an option. They had a mouth equipped with big strong snappers for a reason, and they used stealth and had an ability to fight to survive. When mature, they had massive shells the size of a car steering wheel and were Alpha predators in their underwater environment. With their primal prehistoric temperament that lacked any form of compassion, an individual did not want to have a snapper's flesh cutting, bone snapping jaws anywhere close to them.

Blossom had watched her six ducklings grow quickly. The downy fluff was gone, replaced by dull brown feathers. They were not yet taking on the coloration of their parents, but they would before their first breeding season, including blue wing patches, and curled up feathers on the drakes' tails. They were now testing out their flying capability, half paddling and flying as they moved around the pool. In a month, they would not need her constant help, and she would allow them to fend for themselves. They needed to learn and move on beyond the pond as soon as they could fly, as its space and food supply could not support this many mature ducks. They would need to forage at other ponds, nearby grain fields, streams, rivers, and lakes that offered a greater variety and quantity of food. This increased mobility would also allow them the safety advantages that larger water areas provided against land animals and two leggers.

In only four months they would move toward the coast and join other mallards, waterfowl, and temperate climate land birds to travel south to warmer latitudes, as their water world and food supply here would be solidly encased with ice. In that migration period, Blossom would need to find a new mate for the next breeding season. If nothing fatal happened to her, she expected to return to this little water oasis to nest and raise another group of ducklings.

For now, she still needed to help her youngsters increase their situational awareness and ability to stay alert. She gave a warning quack as she spotted Rusty, one of the local foxes, trying to get within striking distance of one of Blossom's young, it was perched on a log next to the water, proudly preening his new feathers and not paying attention to his surroundings. He heard her warning and launched off into the water, foiling any possibility of becoming lunch for Rusty's young kits and mate Rosa back at the den. Rusty stopped his unsuccessful approach, sat up, started scratching behind his ear, then gave a snort and moved back into the tree line.

Next time, check for lookouts, and plan your approach accordingly, he noted to himself.

Legs, in true bull frog indifference, had quietly observed the young duck's potential demise while resting her feet on the bottom of the pond, her spotted greenish-brown head and expressionless black pupil eyes poking just out of the algae-covered water. She was cool, calm, and collected whenever Beak or Knees, the blue herons, were not hanging around looking to have frog sushi.

Legs' bull frog thinking, and attitude were just fine as far as Cuddles was concerned. He continued to slowly glide up the underwater slope, eyeing Legs' pair of smooth, muscular finned limbs hanging below the pond's skylit surface.

Chapter 5
The Attack

It was the last Friday in May, and in less than three weeks, school would be out for the summer. The ten-foot-tall tree in the courtyard just outside Mrs. Dean's classroom windows now had twenty little green apples. Each apple still had the remnants of a dried blossom that had once held beautiful white and pink petals and was surrounded by a cluster of shiny dark green leaves with a white velvet-like fuzz underneath. This was the first time a large group of apples had grown on this tree. Mrs. Dean told the class that it was a Red Delicious apple tree and that possibly in the fall, when they were in the third grade and the apples had matured and ripened, they might be able to pick them and taste them and confirm if they were indeed red and delicious.

For Mrs. Dean and her students, however, the tree was not just about apples. It was also about birds. From one of the larger branches hung a wire cage holding suet, while another main branch held a bird feeder platform. There was also a double crook black iron holder with a suet cage hanging on one crook and another bird seed filled feeder platform swinging from its twin.

13

Each school day, the platform feeders were replenished by Mrs. Dean's class. Because the suet cakes were greasy and hard to handle, Helen filled the empty wire holders herself, thereby avoiding a white slime from being deposited by little hands on every door, hallway, and classroom surface between the feeders and the bird food storage bin. Helen loved seeing the birds outside her school window, just like she loved watching them outside her kitchen window at home; except here there were no squirrels or chipmunks climbing the feeders in the school courtyard. Best of all, she enjoyed seeing her students learn more about the birds and witnessing their increased ability as a class to identify the distinct species.

A wide variety of bird species were attracted to the feeders. Bird books were kept in a special rack on the windowsill ledge, so when an unknown bird was seen, the students could do their own research to learn its name, where it nested, the type of nest it made, the color and number of its eggs, its unique call and behaviors, and its range of territory at different times of the year.

One day when Helen had pointed out that different birds ate specific types of seeds plus other foods like worms and bugs, Lyra had asked, "Can we feed them pizza? Everyone loves pizza!" Led by Russell, the rest of the class chanted, "Pizza! Pizza! Pizza! Pizza!" Helen had laughed with the glee of her own inner child, exuding pure joy. So distinctive was her laugh that she was often recognized well before she was seen. This was often the case, as she was just over five foot tall.

Raising the hand signal for the students to be silent, she squelched the short-lived celebration and crescendo of the pizza chorus. Smiling, she explained that pizza would not be good for the birds, and it would also attract non-native species like starlings, with their long sword-like yellow beaks that they readily used as a weapon to attack other birds and to eat their eggs and their babies. "They are one of the best examples of an invasive species. Starlings, along with English sparrows, were introduced by lovers of Shakespeare in Central Park in New York City. Although not intentionally meaning to do it, bringing these European birds to North America had a devastating impact on many native songbirds across all the lower forty-eight states plus farther north in Alaska and Canada."

"Who is Shakespeare?" asked Trisa. Helen chuckled, realizing she sometimes forgot she was talking to second graders. "A man who wrote some famous plays a long time ago," she responded. "Oh," was all Trisa said in response, obviously not interested in learning more about Shakespeare. Helen laughed inwardly, deciding that talking about the invasion of the Beatles from England would not be appreciated by Trisa or the rest of the class either. Moments like those were what made teaching so special for her.

The two students assigned to bird feeder duty that day were Danielle and Randy. Danielle was a very timid child who originally would never ask for help, and who never seemed comfortable with how she fit in with other students. Helen had paid close attention to Danielle once she realized that the girl was not advancing at the same pace as her classmates. Helen had made it a point to give Danielle simple opportunities to ask questions, and she let her know that she was not alone in not understanding some things. Danielle was making progress, but more was needed.

Danielle's shyness had slowly been replaced with courage, which sprouted more confidence to ask questions in front of the class. Learning, Helen realized, was a constant journey of small victories to comprehension, overcome setbacks; some triumphs are known and others unknown, but still all victories, progress, and growth.

With the school year now almost over, Helen felt like she should have done more, as she thought of them as her own kids, not just assigned students, and she wanted them to thrive.

Randy's autism per his transcript from California ranged between moderate and severe. Erma Bennett, who was the EA hired for his case, along with the special education team, had worked with him, and he had become more comfortable in the classroom. When he was obviously stressed, Randy had problems communicating and expressed frustration with his body motions.

On two separate occasions, Randy had become very animated and was not able to speak clearly, so Erma had removed him from the classroom and calmed him down. Both times, the perceived issue had fortunately been identified and resolved once he could be understood. To the class's credit, they had all been kind to him and included him in their activities and play where possible.

Erma was with Randy and Danielle as they picked up the bucket of birdseed and the scoop for filling the feeders from the storage container that protected the seed from mice. They proceeded out of the room and down the hallway to the right, around the corner to the glass door leading out to the courtyard. Randy had done this job before, and he had been paired with Danielle because it appeared he was more relaxed when around her. In fact, he wanted to carry the bucket and let her fill all the feeders. Chivalry was not dead in second grade, oddly enough, thanks to a young man with autism.

As they stepped through the doorway, the late spring air enveloped them with soft, moist warmth. Today was a good day for bird feeder duty and escaping from the classroom. That was not always so.

On days when it was raining or bitterly cold, they opened a window adjacent to the apple tree and just tossed the birdseed out. When it snowed, however, they still went out to fill the feeders, as they had a very supportive and caring team of school custodians who would shovel a path to the feeders so that Helen's little people could do their task. No shoveling or tossing was required on this day, and the bright warm embrace felt good.

Danielle started with the feeder hanging on the iron crook. Erma noticed Randy looking at her with an unusually bright smile as he held the bucket out so she could dig out a scoop of seed. Danielle smiled back. Erma watched the little team perform their job well.

As Danielle got a second scoop of seed and headed to the feeder in the apple tree, Randy became agitated. Looking up at Erma, trying but unable to speak, he started stomping. He frowned, appearing terrified and ready to cry. His body was shaking and with his free hand he was waving and pointing his finger in Danielle's direction. Randy obviously wanted Erma to do something, but what? *Does he want to fill the last feeder?*

Suddenly, Randy bolted toward Danielle as she was about to put the seed into the feeder. "Oh no!!" Erma exclaimed as she saw Randy sling all the seed in the bucket, hitting the unsuspecting Danielle in the back with a hard, targeted explosion, hurting and scaring her.

"What did I do to you?" the little girl cried, tears beginning to flow down her quivering dark brown cheeks.

Why the unprovoked attack when things were going so well? Was he smiling earlier because he was already celebrating his planned sneak attack on poor Danielle? Erma was shocked at how quickly things had changed in Randy's demeanor. He appeared to be happy with himself for what he had done.

She quickly grabbed the bucket out of Randy's hand, then bent down to Danielle and asked her if she was ok. Her timidness was back, her lower lip trembling as she latched onto Erma's arm. "It's ok, sweetie. Randy is not going to hurt you again," Erma assured her.

Lifting the little girl to her hip, and with her other hand holding the bucket handle and Randy's hand, she headed back inside. She would let Mrs. Dean know what happened and would likely have to meet with Randy's special needs case manager. Erma was bewildered and flustered now. *What had triggered Randy's violent behavior?* she kept asking herself. Thank goodness it was just birdseed and not the bucket he had thrown, but it was still a deliberate and planned act of aggression against such a sweet, innocent child.

Chapter 6
Paradise

With her ducklings now self-sustaining, flying, and venturing out independently, Blossom was free to explore away from the beaver pond on her own. Swimming around, she decided to take to the air, and soon she was flying over Marble Brook School. Looking down, she noted that there was a large puddle of water on the flat roof, left from the prior day's thunderstorm. Feeling like she deserved some time at the spa, she circled over the building and not seeing any hazards, cupped her wings and glided down to the rooftop pool. As she passed over the school courtyard, Blossom spied a small pile of yellow and gold material scattered under the apple tree that grew next to the building. Splashing down in the sun-warmed pool of water (or as known in avian circles, a duck hot tub), she enjoyed the relaxing sensation of the water's soothing heat on her webbed feet and legs. Curious as to what she had seen on her approach, she bobbled over to the roof's edge, overlooking the courtyard, all the while keeping a wary 360-degree eye for Nails and her kindred raptors.

Peering down, she was pleased to see that the yellow and

golden material she had glimpsed was a scattered pile of seed, a virtual all-you-can-eat-buffet, left by Randy when he attacked Danielle. The school's daytime residents had come and gone, no children's voices could be heard, and the courtyard was quiet and appeared to be empty of any occupants. Blossom quietly slipped down over the roof's edge and hovered to a soft landing on the grass below. Being an unfamiliar space with its surrounding brick walls and tall sets of windows and doors, Blossom was hesitant to move from her landing spot. Her muscles remained tensed in case she spotted an immediate threat and needed to spring back skyward and escape.

Fortunately, nothing moved in the courtyard, and she gradually relaxed, although she remained wary. She soon realized that this was a unique peaceful place with trees and shrubs that provided shade and cover around the edges of the yard, with one larger tree toward the middle of the wall-surrounded area, along with a stone bench and concrete pad on one side, with sidewalks connecting it to the doorways. The rest of the area was clipped green grass. Blossom slowly moved toward the scattered seed, peering around and under the shrubs and trees for hidden predators. To her relief, nothing moved. It appeared she had the whole courtyard to herself. *Wow! What a find!*

Approaching the seed, she eyed a pan of water, tucked next to a holly bush. *Shelter, food, water, and no predators! What an amazing place! Is this the answer to my dreams?* With these happy thoughts, Blossom enjoyed some nourishment, then sipped water from the pan to wash down her wonderful all-she-could-eat-buffet meal.

With her croup stretched full, Blossom was content, and she spent the late afternoon cautiously moving around the courtyard. She traveled along the shrubs on the outer perimeter and found nothing, not even a mouse. Not only was Marble Brook's spa relaxing, the restaurant, accommodations, and security all seemed to be five stars. Like anyone a unknown place, she liked having strong physical barriers between her and any potential intruders. Blossom found herself thinking, *Perhaps I will stay here for the night.* She moved over and settled down under a line of thick-trimmed shrubs on the south side of the yard.

As the orange clouds and blue sky faded to dark magenta above, Blossom noticed that lights would periodically come on in each classroom around the courtyard, and when they did, she saw a two-legged being with featherless wings move slowly around the classroom, occasionally dipping down and back up. It carried a long snouted noise maker, pushing the snout around objects in the room. Curious about what it was trying to scare out of the room, Blossom waited to see what might escape or happen. Besides light and noise, nothing presented itself.

As the two-legged creature moved around the courtyard perimeter classrooms, Blossom positioned herself on the opposite side. Eventually, in the middle of the night, the two legger, lights, and noise maker disappeared, leaving a peaceful quiet, except for the super ducks flying very high that were creating straight clouds to mark their paths. She had always wondered where the super ducks nested, and whether the legend that she heard during her stay down south last winter of a flame-throwing "Killer Duck" was true. Some claimed they had seen one up close, but Blossom had only observed the super ducks and truth be known, she was happy to not meet a fire-breathing killer.

Not seeing any direct threats since she had arrived, Blossom settled down in the moonlight shade of a shrub and took a nap till the morning. Really it was a half of a nap, as her duck brain allowed her to sleep with one eye open, so she traded between each eye over the course of the night without any activity or creatures seen or heard, except for the occasional hum of a night-time insect.

At first light she heard other birds start their singing, and then she saw them swoop into the suet in the bird feeders that hung above the spilled seed on the ground. Downey, Hairy, and the red-bellied woodpeckers were joined by nuthatches, chickadees, crested titmice, and a pair of cardinals. Having filled up the night before, Blossom ambled over to the seed, took a few bites, and then a refreshing sip of cool water. *What a nice start to the day.*

Besides the birds, the courtyard and school remained quiet and peaceful all day. As night approached, she anticipated the return of the lights and two-legged noise maker, but nothing happened. The seed on the ground was almost gone on the second day, but still the courtyard remained quiet and safe, with only songbirds and an occasionally raucous crow flying over the school.

In late afternoon, Blossom decided to stretch her wings and leave her newly found refuge to find some food in the river that flowed along the base of the hill. Flying above a tall but narrow dam, she landed in the middle of the pond and slowly paddled over to a sandy island, scooping up small pebbles to help her digest the seeds she had eaten the night before. She then started foraging for tender plants, algae, and bugs in the shallow water's edge and overhanging plants on the stream bank.

As a light drizzle began to fall, Blossom could hear motor vehicles passing on the nearby road above the pond's bank. Soon the tires made a swishing noise as they threw up spray from the road's surface, and their red and white lights flashed by through the brushy undergrowth that bordered the riverside road.

Having satiated her appetite with water plants and various water creatures that were full of protein, Blossom thrust her wings hard into the river water's surface; this lifted her body up so it broke free of the water's suction. This allowed her wings to raise her up into the grey drizzle so she could return to her newly found refuge at the Marble Brook spa and enjoy another quiet night of rest.

Circling the school in the fading light, she saw that the wet parking lot was free of any cars and buses. All appeared quiet below. Unseen, she glided into a soft landing on the roof, did a quick peek over the roof's edge at the courtyard, and seeing the area deserted except for a pair of cardinals below the bird feeders, she quietly hovered down to the ground of her new-found paradise, settling down once again under one of the shrubs.

Chapter 7
Year End

Marble Brook staff and students enjoyed a break over the Memorial Day long weekend. Helen and her husband spent a day and night at a Back Bay hotel in Boston. They visited the New England Aquarium, where Helen refreshed her love for the oceans and their residents. They finished the day by shopping along Newbury Street and having dinner at Legal Sea Foods. With their three children grown and on their own, they were taking more opportunities to get away together.

On Memorial Day Monday, Helen compiled her students' year-end scores from tests and projects and finished the comments on their progress reports so that she could hand them in to Principal Booker the next day. She was working on the last day of her holiday. However, with an overcast sky, a drizzle that started late morning, and a wonderful Boston getaway to boot, she did not mind. She was also updating an action plan for Randy, who fortunately had not had any more incidents since the one with Danielle. In the brief time he had been with them, Erma had done a great job with Randy, and it was expected she would move to third grade with him. She would miss Erma next year. Having another adult in the classroom provided flexibility on supervision coverage plus, like other EA's Helen had had before, Erma was a blessing to know and be around each day.

Helen began reviewing what she would be doing in class over the last two and a half weeks of school. There would be a field trip to the Peabody Museum on Thursday to see the dinosaur skeletons, so she would have to send out permission slips as well as touch base with the parents to coordinate who the chaperones would be. She also needed to schedule a celebration for the students who had a birthday in June and during the summer break. Having a class with a number of allergies always made snack planning a major challenge.

The long-range forecast was calling for the last full week of school to have high humidity and temperatures running into the mid-nineties. From desk height to the ceiling, her classroom wall facing the courtyard was made up of windows that caught the direct sunlight from mid-morning until late afternoon. Room temperatures could rise to 104 degrees Fahrenheit by dismissal time on days where outside temps reached into the nineties. The American Civil Liberties Union would not allow a convicted mass murderer to be incarcerated in this type of conditions, much less confine that person with twenty-two second graders in a relatively small space. She needed to ensure her three handheld battery powered water mister fans were ready to go. For this surely would be a day where the students would be sticking to their desks, papers, and anything else their little sweat soaked clothes and bodies touched. Her only hope to enable them to still learn was to give them frequent mist breaks to cool their crimson-colored faces. Summer break—or an unexpected cold front—could not come soon enough.

Chapter 8
The Break

Blossom was a little unnerved on the fourth morning in her new paradise when big, noisy yellow objects rumbled up to the school and expelled a long string of small two-leggers, and then rumbled away. Earlier, smaller multi-colored objects had move onto the white-striped area, where they stopped and discharged much larger two-leggers. Blossom wondered why the much bigger yellow objects held hatchling two leggers and the smaller multi-colored objects held the full-grown two leggers. She thought it should have been the other way around. Soon windows creaked; then were slammed open allowing the chatter of students to be heard all around the courtyard.

A doorway opened, and a big two legger appeared and started using something on the shrubs that cut off twigs and leaves, and then took a big wide claw and collected the trimmings into piles, which were put into big black bubbles that sat on the ground but never popped.

Blossom was not very happy with the change in paradise, but the two legger did not appear to see her. She moved very slowly around the perimeter of the courtyard to the opposite end, always

26

keeping a shrub or tree trunk between her and the unwelcomed intruder. When the two-legged creature bent over to fill another black bubble, she took to the air and flew straight up and over the roof's edge, gaining height as she circled over the parking lot filled with cars and a cluster of little two leggers out playing on the black surface next to the building.

Blossom then set her course for the nearby beaver pond. There she found Petals and two others of her offspring all sitting and preening their feathers on the fallen tree trunk on the pond's edge. They were looking grown up, but they were still not fully filled out yet, nor did they have their final adult colors that would appear after their first molt.

She glided overhead and gave them a chortled greeting, then glided into the light morning breeze. With her wings gracefully cupped, she descended to land with a relaxing slide into a bubbly stop at the center of the pond in front of them. Petals was glad to see Blossom, and she immediately slid off the log into the water and swam out to greet her.

Petals was a beautiful soft looking young hen with a very strong bond to her mother. The two drakes on the other hand were too busy fussing with their looks, not knowing that it would be next year before they would reach sexual maturity and have their green heads and white stripe around their necks. Not that they really cared about attracting a mate yet, as they were full of themselves at this point, but Blossom was sure the young males would in time become handsome drakes like their long-gone dad.

Blossom enjoyed the balance of the day foraging with her offspring and observing them. The three ducklings took to the air when a two legger tossed a stick into the pond and his dog exploded into the water to retrieve it. It was pure joy for her to wing up over the trees with them, swerve around each other, and land back on the pond when the dog and the two legger had moved on. The day passed quickly, and the daylight waned. She decided to return to Marble Brook, where only two rumblers now sat. Lights were on in two rooms, one of which faced the courtyard.

Landing on the roof, she investigated the yard below; she could hear a noise maker whirring from one of the lit rooms. There was nothing happening in the courtyard, not even any cardinals at the feeders, so she descended into her new sanctuary. Waddling over to the bird feeders, she enjoyed the unwanted millet that had been tossed by the finches when digging for Nyjer seed. She took a sip of water from the pan, pulled her beak up, and then she leisurely strolled toward the shrubs on the south side of the yard. The big black bubbles were now gone. The longer new growth stems from the shrubs having been sheared off by the big two legger, they now appeared neatly squared on top, bottom, and sides. Despite the trim, the foliage was still thick enough to block the light and hungry eyes from above.

As was the pattern the first night she had been there, the noise from inside soon ended, all lights around the courtyard were turned off and the quiet night settled in. A contented Blossom rested.

So far, the camouflage of her brown feathers, along with her cautiousness, had allowed her to come and go without any detection by the two leggers. Most mornings, soon after the large yellow moving objects had unloaded their passengers, a pair of little two-legged creatures and sometimes a big two legger would come into the courtyard carrying something containing seed, which they used to fill the feeders.

Blossom was almost discovered one of the first mornings there when she decided to snack on some spilled cracked corn kernels. Fortunately, she was able to move away to a corner shrub before being seen. Blossom had remained still and did not panic, and her presence remained a secret. After observing this daily occurrence for three days, Blossom developed a routine of flying away at the first sound of rumblers, then returning in the evening when almost all of them as well as the two leggers were gone.

The school year ended on a warm muggy day, and Helen and

her peers were ready for the summer break. The office staff and custodians, along with the summer-school teachers and their students, were now the only people in the building. The sports fields still had some activity but mostly for travel teams, not the large groups that usually participated with the town's little league and soccer programs. Helen was now free to enjoy days and evenings catching up on family projects and visits with friends and relatives. She could spend her evenings on other activities besides lesson planning.

What changed? Blossom wondered. She still felt this was the place she had dreamed of for incubating and raising her ducklings, safe and secure from the predators that had caused her so much grief and worry back at the beaver pond, but since it was not nesting season and there was also no fresh seed to attract her, she dropped into Marble Brook only a few times over the rest of the summer, each time finding the courtyard quiet, and no seed in or around the feeders or apple tree. There were just a few vehicles arriving and not many little two leggers inside most days. As the summer wore on, she began to question if finding the seed before had only been a fluke, and maybe this might not be the ideal spot after all.

Chapter 9
New School Year

The summer break had been exciting. Helen and her husband traveled to Ireland with Helen's mother Louise and two of their three children, their daughter Kaye, and their youngest son Michael. Their oldest son Jaime had chosen to stay at home and work. Except for their first night in the land of shamrocks when they stayed at a hotel, the rest of their nights were spent in bed and breakfasts scattered from Dublin in the east to Shannon in the west. The casual country atmosphere in the B&Bs gave them a better sense of the people and culture.

They had prepared to be rained on every day, but they lucked out with dry weather the whole trip. Her husband James went fly fishing for trout with Michael on a tributary of Lake Killarney and came back with hilarious reports of bouncing sheep. They had seen cartoons where sheep bounced around on all four legs, like they had literal springs for legs, bong, bong, bong. But now they had seen real sheep springing across the Irish pastures.

Their family entourage also made it to see and kiss the blarney stone, which they agreed was not a healthy activity and might be the cause of a global pandemic someday. Their itinerary took them to visit Limerick Castle, where there was a collection of native wild animals that included a highland stag plus five young half-grown ducks that kept diving and surfacing in their little pool area as they and other tourists stood near the fenced-in enclosure and tried to take pictures.

They had enjoyed standing on the Dingle Peninsula ridgeline as the clouds of cool mist came up from the ocean shoreline below, flowing around them and over the pass. Some people had brought kites and were flying them along the ridgeline's rocky crest.

As they moved on in a rush to capture all they could, they asked an old gentleman walking along the road for directions to the Cliffs of Moher. Upon reflection they realized how rude they had been. It was a missed opportunity to learn about the people and not just see things. The elder gentlemen wearing his tweed coat, vest and tam stopped and kindly entertained their inquiry for help. His thick brogue made it hard for them to understand his English. They wished we had taken the time and asked him about life there. But they didn't, their loss, mistake.

At the Cliffs of Moher, with their precipitous rock ledges facing the sea, they watched the sea birds far below whirl and call as they landed on ledges where they had roosts and nests. The birds would then launch back off the cliff's rock balconies and soar on the updrafts of the salty air and mist as they raced up from the cold ocean waves. The moistened air floated up and caught the land breeze that took it over the cliffs' edge to settle and be breathed in by the green mowed fields. The pasture land was segmented by dark lichen covered stone fences, forming a quilted landscape which pushed up the slope of its own shadowed wave to crest at the peak of the seaward cliffs that met and held up the sunset's glorious sky.

One night while in Killarney, Helen and her husband went to the local pub for dinner and listened to the Irish music, while Kaye and Michael went out on their own to explore the town. They saw an elderly woman at a table, surrounded by her clan of middle-aged children and their spouses, who were there to celebrate her birthday. The group sang along with the Irish band, the birthday girl being the loudest. Her young male subjects took turns taking her to the floor to dance an Irish jig, which she did with the same exuberance and delight as she sang. It was infectious watching this family create their own craic.

Time slipped by quickly. It was much later than they originally planned when they returned to the small B&B. Their lodging was nestled in an area of homes on the edge of the town center. Both kids were back from their night's adventure. Michael was in bed already, but he was not the least bit settled. Apparently in a moment of musical inspiration engendered by someone named Guinness, "A quite stout guy," Michael had claimed with a warmed smile, he had purchased a cheap set of bag pipes. With a comical face and raised left eyebrow, he was happily playing his rendition of what must have been the "Ode to a Dying Whale," in the key of "B" for bad.

Indeed, their vacation was a memorable one, especially with Louise able to join them. She had hoped to travel with her husband Clyde, but unfortunately, he had become ill soon after retiring from his forty-plus-year military career and could not travel, and he had passed away not long after. Helen and James had hoped this trip would provide her with some of the experience she had looked to share with him. Louise indeed had served her nation too, raising five children on her own most of the time, as Clyde was often deployed when the kids were young. They had lived on both coasts, and also in Brazil and Japan. She was mentally tough indeed, yet so loving and gentle in her manner. Her family's endearing name for her was "Lamb" and with her full, soft snow-white head of hair, the moniker was spot on.

With summer holidays behind her, Helen had attended the district wide convocation at the high school auditorium that kicked off the new school year for staff and administrators. The Marble

Brook PTO had also provided a very nice breakfast for them at the school.

She had already been in her room several times over the past few weeks of August to prepare it, create name plates for each student desk and arrange them. One day her two best friends, one a retired teacher herself, helped her put up a new bulletin board—a requirement of Mrs. Booker. Located in the hallway just outside her door, the board would welcome her new students, represented by stars, who would form the class constellation in only three days. The silver stars with each student's name written in black stood out boldly against the background of dark blue butcher paper.

She checked the birdseed bin and determined she would need to stop by a feed or box store and pick up more, as well as suet cakes to start the year. She would be asking parents to help provide bird seed and suet blocks at the school open house. The students would come on Wednesday for a three-day week. Then on Labor Day Monday, each elementary school would invite students to march with the faculty in the annual parade down Main Street, past the flagpole, and around to King Street. That would make for a four-day week so that the students and teachers could ease into the new school year before facing the usual five-day schedule.

No matter how good the summer break had been, the return of the school year filled Helen with excitement but also fear of what her class, parents, and teaching challenges would be and the lingering fear that she might not be up to it. She got butterflies in her stomach, just like the ones she used to feel before gymnastic competitions in high school. The first of August seemed to be a mental trigger and emotional signal that time was short.

Chapter 10
The Drill

School safety drills had once been strictly about evacuating students in case a fire occurred, or perhaps in rare instances when there was some sort of chemical or gas leak. When she was little and the Cold War nuclear arms race with Russia was in full swing, Helen and her classmates had practiced moving into a center hallway in case there was a nuclear attack. Despite the drill, most everyone doubted that if there was such an attack, sitting down with your head between your knees was going to help much.

The April 1999 Columbine High School shooting changed that. Visitors now had to request permission to enter the school building at an intercom with a camera mounted next to the front door entrance, then be granted access by someone in the office who would remotely open the lock. Most likely any intruder at an elementary school would not be an upset nine-year-old student, but rather a disgruntled spouse who wanted to see or take their child they had lost custody of in some family court.

The local volunteer fire department, an insurance company representative, and other officials had to observe and critique evacuations; although, they did all recognize that a planned drill was not like an actual emergency where chaos and lack of information often ruled. Nevertheless, that day at ten a.m. sharp the fire alarm would sound, and students would line up at their door; leave the classroom, proceed to the nearest outside exit, then march single file up the entrance road to the firehouse on the corner. Once there, teachers would then assemble their class in the parking lot to verify that all their students were present and await instructions for them to return to the school building. Thankfully, the possibility of having to evacuate the school was extremely low.

Chirp! Chirp! Chirp! Helen instructed her students to stop what they were doing, and they all left the room and proceeded to their designated evacuation exit door. Helen was a rule follower. Per school's work rules she did not carry her cell phone during the day, as the administrators believed that a select few would spend their day texting, and not teaching. Her phone was stowed with her purse in the classroom closet and was therefore, left behind. When everyone had exited the room, Helen closed the door behind her, but she did not waste time locking it, as it would require her to use a key; this prevented students from locking teachers out of the classroom, which was more likely than needing to isolate students in a classroom, away from a threat. She then moved up to the head of her line of students as they began their trek out into the parking lot and on down the entrance roadway to the firehouse.

What a curious sight, thought Blossom as she flew back toward the beaver pond to see how things were with her family. She had been on the river with a few other ducks, enjoying the mild late summer weather and the bountiful supply of high protein biomass that it provided. *Those two-leggers are acting just like us with our ducklings,* she observed. *All following in a line with a grown two-legger at their side leading them away from the school building. I wonder why they decided to swarm today. Where could they all be going?* Blossom puzzled, flying higher above the school so it was easier to watch as more and more clusters emerged. *Wow! There are bunches of them now. Maybe they are starting a migration of their own, or did something scare them out of their big nest? I should not go to the courtyard tonight just in case whatever frightened them is still there,* she reasoned.

The groups of two leggers eventually merged onto the path used by the rumblers that cut through a tall stand of pine trees. They looked just like sheep she had seen going through a gate as they began to split off into smaller clusters, moving into an open area where they all stopped in their little groups. She took one last look at the two-legger throng, and then banked away from the scene. She easily glided on toward the beaver pond.

Chapter 11
Getting Together

With the summer heat having peaked, there was movement on the warm sandy loam of the pond embankment as a cluster of juvenile snappers pushed up to the surface, using their little front legs to scoot their way down the slope to the pond's warm water. The growing season was over halfway done and Blossom, along with other ducks and geese, needed to build up her fat reserves on insects, snails, and other high protein aquatic foods plus start taking advantage of residual grain left in fields that were now being cut down by two leggers sitting on big green and red equipment.

The breeding season and raising her ducklings had not allowed Blossom to keep up her own nourishment, so the next few months were critical to restore her energy reserves and body fat. She was also vulnerable now as she molted and replaced her old feathers, and during this period there would be many days where she would not be able to fly. Having a good diet determined how well her feathers would grow back and the amount of thermal protection she would have in the months ahead as ponds, streams, and then lakes froze over. In those conditions, they would all be forced to find refuge in limited areas of open freshwater rivers and lakes and in coastal estuaries, where there was an increasing scarcity of healthy food sources, such as high protein insects. This was compounded by the concentration of other hungry beaks looking for nourishment in those same areas.

As the annual cycle of life progressed toward cold weather, more mallards from the upper continent region would begin to gather in increasing numbers. With this came shared experience, a form of avian informational crowdsourcing. The combined knowledge, along with a larger number of eyes to spot threats, would pay benefits and increase the collective survival chances for all the ducks, especially for young mallards. Blossom and her grown offspring would join this movement and follow the celestial markers, magnetic field, and topography to their winter destination.

With her brood no longer dependent on her, Blossom could also focus on finding a new mate for the coming year. She would have to fend off various suitors who outnumbered the hens to find a dependable drake. The courtship would last through the early winter months and, if successful, he would follow her in the spring to wherever she built her nest. This time she hoped it would not be at the little beaver pond, but rather the courtyard at her Marble Brook spa and paradise.

Chapter 12
One School, One Read

Today was the school assembly for the One School, One Read announcement. Principal Booker had introduced the program to emphasize literary arts and just as importantly, to create a shared experience across the school and the extended Marble Brook community. It would be one large book club made up of students, parents, and other family members for the next four weeks.

The chosen book title had been a closely guarded secret that only Mrs. Glover, the Literary Arts specialist, knew, along with Principal Booker and Sally Fiske, a third-grade teacher. Peggy had observed some of Sally's fine artwork and knowing she had also minored in graphic design as an undergraduate student in college, had asked her to reproduce the cover of the book on a foam board. The book cover now sat on a spotlighted easel that was covered by a red satin cloth on the center right area of the stage. Every student and teacher would receive a personal copy of the book to read and keep. Book bundles, double wrapped in brown paper and delivered that morning to each classroom, sat unopened on each teacher's desk until after the announcement.

Mrs. Glover was the first person on the stage. She wore a pair of well-pressed dress slacks that had sharp creases front and back and her trademark turtleneck sweater and vest with large pockets. Her demeanor communicated confident authority as she walked up to the microphone stand and gave the "silence" sign, and the gathered assembly quieted down after the obligatory coughs that seemed to be mandatory before students could listen.

"Welcome everyone to this year's One-School, One-Read introduction celebration. Again, this year we have found an excellent book that I know you will enjoy. Before we announce the title, we have a very special guest, an author I think you will find most interesting. I am certain that you will recognize some of the characters she has created. She lives nearby in the Berkshires and will talk to you about how she was inspired to write about her favorite character. I am pleased to introduce Mrs. Gertrude Carter, who will talk about her friend Tamand."

A buzz ran through the assembly, as most of the students knew the character Tamand as the wise old sage anteater in the Andes rainforest who all the other animals went to for advice on how to deal with problems and unsolved mysteries facing them and other forest creatures. So well-known was Tamand that students often mimicked the character's trademark phrase when he was stroking the chin fur under his long-pointed snout, "So you say my friend. So you sa-a-a-ay." And many of the children were already striking Tamand's contemplative pose.

Gertrude Carter was a short, stout woman with grey streaked hair evenly cut at her shoulders, and a big, infectious smile. She waved to the assembled students as she stepped up to the microphone, greeting them with, "Wow, what a welcome. Hello everyone. Thank you for inviting me here today to talk with you about my good friend Tamand." She then went on to explain how Tamand came to be, inspired by her experience as a little girl living with her missionary parents in Honduras.

The audience was captivated by her enthusiasm as she spoke

about Tamand, and how he represented the best in people and the need for knowledge, and wisdom. She finished by encouraging all of them to be thoughtful listeners and helpful friends. And then she invited everyone to say with her, "So you say my friend. So, you sa-a-a-ay." The audience cheered as Gertrude smiled broadly back at them, then waved goodbye.

With the assembly all revved up, Mrs. Glover invited Principal Booker to join her on stage to reveal the One-School, One Read book. Stepping up to the covered easel, Peggy lifted off the red satin cloth with a matador like flourish, which almost toppled the whole display as the cloth cover caught on the pointed corner of the foam board panel, and then she announced, "This year's One School, One Read is the brand-new *Mystery of the Missing Caterpillars* by Gertrude Carter."

The students cheered and clapped. Peggy directed loudly, "You are now dismissed to go to your rooms and receive your copy of the book. Happy reading, everyone!" Then she paused and said, "Now what do you say students?" The pumped-up assembly postured and shouted back, "So you say my friend, so you sa-a-a-ay." And there was a noisy exit of the cafetorium as the classes clamored out and returned to their rooms.

Chapter 13
Colorful Change

Night temperatures had gradually declined and with that the distinct species of hardwood trees began to put on their seasonal ensembles of color. The maples with their red, orange, and yellow hues began the parade, followed by the beech, walnut, and hickory trees with their bright yellows, along with the dogwoods and sassafras with their blood reds. The oaks held their display until early November, when they presented their dark golden and brown hues to the hillsides' color palate.

With her annual molt well in the past, Blossom sported a new wrap of softly oiled vibrant feathers that only enhanced her appearance, and their luster reflected that she had been successful in maintaining a diet of high protein foods. She was as prepared as she could be for the coming months when her personal survival would be most challenged and conditions most stressful. The sun was still rising high, and most afternoons its warmth was soothing. She enjoyed being able to rest and oil her feathers as she sat either on an exposed log or beach in sun-drenched corners of streams and quiet lake coves.

These restful conditions were especially pleasant, as just a few weeks before there had been some very violent rains and high winds, so strong that they raked the tops off the white capping waves. She had been forced, along with her peers on the lake, to find shelter in protected coves and behind structures. In some spots, the winds had been so powerful that whole hillsides of trees had fallen on top of each other, making the slope look like the slicked down fur of a wet otter. The prolonged battering of the wind, which quieted briefly and then came back in the opposite direction just as hard, had left her addled and a little disoriented. Finally, by nightfall the winds had started to lessen, and the open water had begun to settle down, allowing her to regain her sense of calm and physical stability. The water's edge was full of broken clusters of leaves, which the winds had whipped off the trees. Just in the past few years, there had been two similar events which she never remembered happening before, and she wondered why they were occurring.

As if thinking about change could cause change, she felt the sun's warmth quickly fade. The wind picked up speed, dragging along little ripples across the lake in front of her. The sun was now blocked behind a fast-approaching and lowering line of heavy umber-colored clouds. These were not clouds that produced flashes of light and noise, but they still seemed to be menacing in their appearance and behavior. As they approached, the wind shifted directions, bringing with it a definite chill that felt like it was coming from a frozen lake. As daylight faded, she noticed white flecks of ice pellets falling and floating in the water's surface film. Soon large clusters of wet snowflakes started falling and continued into the night, requiring her to periodically ruffle and shake it off her head and wings. The sounds became muffled as the sticky snow coated grass, leaves, rocks, and the northeast side of tree trunks. The quiet darkness was suddenly replaced by streaking light and a rolling rumble, and the snowfall intensified. This weather was also unfamiliar to her, for it usually occurred only during warm weather periods.

As the night progressed, she began to hear big limbs snapping off the tree trunks. The water laden snow was adding tremendous amounts of weight as it latched onto the colored leaves still clinging to the trees. This occurrence multiplied the snow's leverage on the branch connections to the trunk, doubling or tripling the weight's effect on each limb's base. Each time a large branch yielded with a sharp crack, breaking away and taking smaller ones down with them, it startled her. The long limb sections as they broke away from trunks took other limbs and smaller trees down with them. Blossom soon realized that the shoreline was the wrong place to be. Trees already leaning over the lake to capture more sunlight were especially vulnerable to the added weight. Her move into the open lake was wise, as a half dead maple toppled into the lake exactly where she had been only seconds before.

The storm moved on, and the snowfall rate gradually slowed just as a new day's eastern sky brightened, despite the cloud covered sunrise. The scene was totally different from the day before, as snow clung to everything except the dark surface of the lake. As the clouds cleared and the sun crested the hill, the bright white landscape became blinding to look at, and things were covered with fifteen inches of frozen mush.

The warm October sun returned. The snow sloughed off the leaves, but most of the trees were already severely wounded and splintered, especially taller trees that had slender limbs spreading across the highest level of the forest. These specifically seemed to have uniformly snapped off high in the tree canopy. Their splintered limbs now hung upside down, having shaken off their load of snow, but it was too late to avoid damage. The trees appeared to have been trimmed to a lower height across the forested hills that bordered the lake. It was amazing just how much damage had been done. A snowflake by itself was not that powerful, but the power of many was an overwhelming force that even the strongest oaks could not escape injury.

Chapter 14
The Assignment

Marble Brook's teachers and students were struggling to make up lost time, having missed a total of seven days of school due to a September tropical storm and a freak late October snowstorm. Both weather events had felled trees, knocking power out for multiple days each time. Bus routes were blocked by trees and downed power lines. Local utilities, state, and town crews became overwhelmed in both instances, and lots of grandstanding politicians promised that utilities would pay for their poor response when in truth though, all were to blame because there was a lack of communication and coordination between the organizations and many resources sat idle for days, waiting for assignments for days.

Normally six snow days were to be expected from December through March, but it was only November, and they already exceeded that norm for the school year. If they had a typical winter, the school year might extend to the end of June. Now, Thanksgiving break was upon them before they could catch up. Planning calendars were a mess, and everyone was needing a break to regroup and recharge.

On the first day back from the Thanksgiving holiday, Mrs. Bonnie Hatfield wanted to regain student enthusiasm for writing that the *Mystery of the Missing Caterpillars* had piqued in her students. She gave her third grade class a major writing assignment connected to an activity or event they were involved in that they were proud of and wanted to share. When completed, she planned to post each student's composition on her class's hallway bulletin board for the parent-teacher conferences in mid-December.

Randy Jackson immediately knew what he was going to write about. Since the attack in second grade, Danielle's parents had requested with the support of the staff, her assignment to a different class than him. He missed seeing her in his new class; plus, he missed being able to see and feed the birds, helping them survive through the frigid winter months.

Over the next few days, Mrs. Hatfield reviewed how to write the introduction, body, and conclusion of their stories. Doing this one section at a time helped her assess each child's thought process and writing aptitudes, and it also provided her with one-on-one teaching moments.

Each student author was asked to draft each section for her constructive critique; then, based upon her coaching, they were expected to rewrite it for final review before going on to the next section. Her objective was that every author would have a coherent personal story to share with the class and to post on the bulletin board for parents to read.

Erma was no longer Randy's EA. Her husband lost his job in late October when the global banking crisis had hit the financial services sector hard, and they were forced to move in mid-November, out of state for his new job.

Randy's new EA was Tina Rose, who was still learning the school, their daily schedules, and staff members as well as building a relationship with Randy. This was her first EA assignment, and she was thrilled that it was in third grade, where the students were so sweet and endearing.

Chapter 15
Story Introduction

My *fayrit thin in secund grade was to fead the burds. Karead the burd sead for Danyell. Danyell was vary nice to me. I lik her a lot.* Randy had obviously written the introduction to his story without any assistance. Studying his work, Tina recognized that he was struggling with his spelling but after sounding it out, she could understand his intent. He had very coherent thoughts and was trying to spell words phonetically. His topic was about his favorite thing to do in second grade, which was feeding the birds in Mrs. Dean's class.

Tina had not met Mrs. Dean, but she had seen the bird feeders when she had toured the school courtyard on her recent day of orientation with Mrs. Hatfield. Tina was not sure if Bonnie would want her to edit his work, so she decided not to so she could see where Randy was in his development. It had been explained to her that Randy would get agitated and upset when frustrated, and she was not sure if making corrections or suggestions might trigger such behavior. The notes she had seen on such events had been few, and it was not clear to her what the triggers were without having had a chance to talk to Mrs. Dean, since the former EA was not available to field her questions.

Bonnie used a silent reading period to review each of the story introductions with each child individually. When it was Randy's turn, she discovered that he had several issues with his introductory draft, but there was nothing she had not seen before nor anything unusual for a third grader. He told her he had written it without any help from his parents. The next open house was still three weeks away, so she did not have a feel for the situation at home and his level of parental support. To get a feel for his home support, she would tell him to ask his parents to help him make the changes.

Randy seemed to understand the instructions she gave him but never really looked at her during their exchange. He kept staring at the paper while his right hand bounced on his right leg. He was obviously experiencing some emotion or nervousness, which was not unusual to see, even with neuro-typical kids.

Later, when all the students had gone home, Bonnie touched base with Tina on Randy's day and his progress on his story introduction's revisions. Tina asked if it was all right if she talked to Mrs. Dean about Randy's past behaviors. Bonnie thought it a particularly good idea and suggested they set up a meeting as soon as possible.

Chapter 16
A Mate

Blossom and her remaining offspring had joined with the greater mallard nation in early December just off the Raritan River outlet to the Atlantic at Sandy Hook, New Jersey. It was a beautiful place for them to migrate, with Barnegat Bay to the south, a lighthouse on the north side shore, and the upper end of Long Beach Island on the opposite side of the bay. Adjacent to the island was a large salt marsh that had been set aside as the Barnegat National Wildlife Refuge. Millions of waterfowl and shore birds moved through this area each year as they migrated to and from their winter destinations.

The courting ritual of the drakes pursuing her as a mate followed a similar script of display, body movements, and physical contact. It was really a combination of things she considered in her search. Blossom could tell the younger ones were more aggressive and lacked confidence. They were all about getting her attention, quacking as loudly and as often as they could while bumping into her. They did not impress her much nor did they have the presence or stronger voice of a mature male. Indeed, her mate should be handsome, but she liked a mate that not only looked good but could handle other suitors with little more than a look to back them off.

She saw him at first hanging back behind the noisy group, splashing and circling around her. When he quacked and bent his neck down into the water with his beak pulled up, creating a perfect little spray of water droplets, she knew he was different and experienced. When he made a low whistle sound, she could tell he was not concerned about the other suitors; his focus was on her, and her alone. She liked that. She liked that a lot.

Seeing she was looking at him past the others, he raised up to display his iridescent dark purplish green head, broad densely feathered burgundy colored breast, and exceptionally black, curly tail feathers. The deep blue wing badges really looked good on him. He dipped his head several times down into the water, flicking little droplets of water into the air, coupled with that soulful low whistle. He was talking to her, and she was enjoying his interest in her. He rocked back and forth as he continued to create little diamonds of water droplets with his bill.

She was pretty sure he was the one, but she was not about to reveal her feelings too quickly. He needed to show some level of commitment to ensure that he was serious about her, so she did not go to him. He soon understood that she wanted to be wooed, so he needed to approach her.

Disappointed but not defeated, he slowly made his way to her, muscling through the younger suitors who yielded to his solid presence. As he approached, he coyly turned his beak away from her to show he was not there to attack like her younger suitors but to be friendly, kind, and gentle, yet strong. He was telling her that she was the one for him but respecting that she had a right to accept or reject him. As he got closer, he started to bob up and down as part of a dance as old as time, and she began to bob gently with him in rhythm.

With his beak still pointing away, he was asking her to swim away with him. She let him know the answer was yes by giving him a gentle bite on his shoulder, then they swam off together, leaving the flotilla of splashing, disappointed younger suitors behind. It was love at first bite.

Chapter 17
The Story

Went outsid to the bird feedrs with Danielle and Mrs. Bennett. I held the bukit. Danielle scuped out the seed. Danielle took the seed to a feeder. I saw a hornit on Danielles back. I was afrad it wood sting Danielle. I pointed at the hornit. Mrs. Bennet did nuthing. It was a big hornit. hornits kill. I thro seed at it. The hornit gon. It scared Danielle. I happe Danielle not stung.

Tina could not help but appreciate Randy's effort. As with his introduction, it was clear that he was not receiving any help from his parents and siblings. He still struggled to spell many common words. To his credit, however, he did spell correctly all the words he had originally misspelled in his introduction, and he had even adapted that new knowledge to correctly spell a similar word.

There was no question he was able to learn if given some guidance.

Tina had not found school easy either. Despite that, her parents, especially her mom, had always told her she could do things if she kept trying. She would have given up several times, especially with math, however over time, with encouragement and

52

subsequent success, she had built up the confidence to keep trying until she understood. Knowing this, her mindset had become one that believed that she would succeed again.

Tina had already talked with Bonnie, who asked her to go ahead and help Randy make the necessary corrections, then share the before and after product with her. Randy seemed to be happy about his story and listened to her closely as they worked through the errors in punctuation, grammar, and spelling. When finished, she praised him for his effort and told him to go ahead and draft his conclusion, which he did. She again walked him through the changes. She sensed he was pleased with his work, and it was obvious that he liked the memory of having helped a classmate avoid injury. The story seemed similar to an incident she had read about in Randy's file, and she wondered if Randy's account was fictional and only in his own mind as a coping mechanism. Regardless, it probably wasn't worth talking about, as it was only a class assignment.

Chapter 18
Why?

The first graders had completed making their gingerbread houses, filling the school with an aroma of spice. The fourth-grade classes prepared for their holiday concert, led by music teacher Cindy Wynjenovich. Next week they would perform in the morning for the students and school staff, and then in the evening for their parents. Having two different audiences allowed them to keep the number of people in the cafetorium below the capacity limit set by the town's fire marshal, who was not only a stickler for crowd size. He was also known to do surprise inspections of classrooms and required removal of all the combustible artwork on display.

Today had been an early dismissal day, and tomorrow would be the same, allowing time for parent teacher conferences. Helen had an exceptionally good class of students, and the parents were very supportive. She would need to give four of her student's parents some negative news, but nothing too serious, mostly just course corrections as opposed to hard reversals or corrective action plans. The only downside of the evening was that she had a couple of divorced parents who wanted separate conferences, which required more time and sometimes could pose some tricky discussions if one former partner started criticizing the other.

Abigail Young was on her own tonight to meet with Mrs. Bishop regarding her daughter Danielle. As best she could tell, Danielle seemed to be enjoying school and had not suffered any trauma like she had the prior year. Thankfully, the perpetrator was no longer in her class, and Danielle would only see him in passing. Mrs. Bishop was not so fortunate, and she had a situation where a child's parents and she were not on the same page, much less the same team it appeared, and this had resulted in her running way behind schedule, with another parent still waiting to go in.

So as not to appear to be eavesdropping, Abigail drifted down toward Mrs. Hatfield's class and decided to look at her hallway bulletin board. She was not looking for anyone in particular, but the name Randy Jackson caught her attention. *That's him. The one who attacked Danielle.* The thought sent a chill through her. The bulletin board had the heading "This is My Story." She looked down at Randy's, titled, "Feeding the Birds." *Feeding the birds, sure, more like hitting my Danielle*, she thought, the memory bringing out the raw emotions inside her. Although she was upset, she still wondered what the little monster wrote, so she read on.

What? Oh my, oh my, no. Why didn't Mrs. Dean or someone tell them about this? A hornet. So Randy was not attacking Danielle but protecting her. Oh, poor child, you were helping, not hurting, and we treated you so badly. She caught her breath as her eyes teared, and her heart ached for both children; plus, it brought back a more recent event that hit hard, causing her body to shake. Why keep it a secret? "Why?" Abigail said to herself out loud, then realizing that no one was waiting outside Mrs. Bishop's door, so she hustled back while trying to regain control of her emotions and the tears that rimmed her eyes.

Despite the tight schedule, Helen's parent meetings had proceeded on time. She had noticed Abigail Young across the hallway, standing alone during Helen's last three meetings. As she escorted her last parent couple to the door, she said hello to Abigail and asked how Danielle was doing this year in Mrs. Bishop's class. As soon as their eyes met, she could tell something was not right. "Mrs. Dean, do you have a moment for a question regarding Danielle?" "Sure, I am finished with all my meetings for tonight. What is your question?" Helen responded, with an inquisitive look and some concern, as Abigail's face showed she was struggling to know what to say. "Is Danielle OK?" she inquired.

Abigail was not sure whether to give an update on Danielle or get to the point of her visit. She hesitated, not knowing how best to start, then went ahead and asked, "Was there a reason you did not tell us about the hornet?" Helen was lost, "What hornet?" "The hornet that Randy Jackson knocked off of Danielle last year with the bird seed," Abigail answered, with a hard look that hit Helen like a slap. Helen was stunned by the question and Abigail's expression. For a moment, overwhelmed by Abigail's tone and confused about the revelation which she struggled to understand its origin and context, Helen stood speechless.

Trying to recover, Helen answered, "I was not aware of any hornet. Who told you this?" she inquired, feeling that she herself must have been kept in the dark.

"No one. I read it," said Abigail.

"Read it? Where?"

"On Mrs. Hatfield's bulletin board. It is a story written by Randy Jackson," Abigail replied.

"This is the first time I have heard about a hornet, but I want to find out if it is true. You said it is posted on Mrs. Hatfield's bulletin board?"

"Yes, under Randy's name."

Helen then realized it must relate to Randy's attack on Danielle. She had seen every write-up about the incident and nowhere did she recall anything about a hornet.

"I am sorry for missing that," Helen apologized, not sure yet just what she had missed but feeling like she was guilty of some terrible transgression. Had she failed little Randy and Danielle? The good feelings about the night's meetings were now destroyed.

Helen could not shake the significance of the new information about Randy's incident. The feeling that she had failed two of her children was a punch to the gut.

Abigail then remembered Helen's question about how Danielle was doing. "We almost lost Danielle this summer," she shared, lowering her head with watering eyes. "What happened?" Helen asked, the wave of emotions generated by Abigail sweeping over her too.

"We were taking a family hike when she was stung by a little sweat bee. Danielle complained about something stinging inside her collar but soldiered on to a favorite waterfall we always hike to next to the lake. She seemed alright, but then our son noticed his sister was starting to look different. Her face was swelling, and there was a red rash appearing on her neck and throat. We kept going, but soon Danielle started to have labored breathing, as if her throat was blocked. That is when we saw the little bee inside her collar. Apparently, Danielle had grabbed her neck and in doing that, she smashed the bee. Fortunately, my husband is in good health, so he picked Danielle up and carried her back to the car, running as quickly as he could through the rugged trail." Abigail paused as the fearful memory froze her voice, then finally took in some air, and continued.

"It took us almost twenty minutes to get back to our car, and then another twenty-five minutes to reach the hospital ER. Danielle was turning blue and going limp as ER staff loaded her onto a gurney." Helen could tell that Abigail was seeing the memory vividly, as her body was quivering, and eyes were tear filled.

Abigail took a couple of short gasps to try and regain her composure. "We told the ER nurse what had happened, and they immediately treated Danielle for an anaphylactic reaction. Danielle's system could not handle the venom, causing the severe symptoms, plus there had been other complications that required her to be hospitalized for over a week. She missed the first two weeks of school, so she started the year behind in her work and socially."

"How is Danielle doing now?" Helen asked. "Is she OK?"

Abigail bobbed her head up and down as she pulled a tissue from her purse to dry her eyes and face, then replied "She is doing fine. We have not seen any residual health problems. Mrs. Bishop just told me she is up to date on her assignments and is performing well, and she seems to be well liked and engaged with her classmates."

The tsunami of emotions charged by the information that Abigail had shared tore at Helen's heart, and it raised that ever present fear that she was inadequate.

"Thank God she is alright now," Helen responded. Although not a professional thing to do, Helen immediately hugged the young mother, to comfort them both.

Chapter 19
Smoke Sticks

The mallard flock that Blossom and her new mate had joined, spent the night feeding on soybeans in a field flooded by torrential rains from a slow-moving cold front which had trudged across the mid-Atlantic seaboard. With a bright moon in a sky cleared by the Alberta clipper moving through, they could easily see to eat and cruise up and down the unharvested rows. As the moon was about to set, the sun started to light up the eastern horizon. Sensing that the day was bringing with it much colder temperatures, the flock took advantage of the prevailing north-northwest wind to continue their journey to a warmer latitude. Quacks and chatter broke the morning quiet as they splashed up into the brightening sky, and the sound of their whistling wings faded to the south.

Having flown some forty miles, they approached a large river which was a key milepost along their route. In the distance, they saw an old oxbow lake that still connected to the river on both ends, but the current had shifted away from its mouth, leaving a normally peaceful and quiet backwater. They aimed for the lower end of the island which, with its stand of river cane and tall marsh grass, provided a windbreak with flat, still water not impacted by the white-capped waves the north wind fetched up in the middle of the oxbow.

As the tired flock approached their planned stopping point just off the lower point of the island's peninsula, they glided downwind so that they could make their approach over the ducks and land in an open area where the island's vegetation only allowed the wind to create a low corduroy of ripples on water.

Their wings whistled as they picked up their wing strokes to pound through the headwind. Blossom decided not to drop down lower with the flock, as she thought the swimming ducks seemed to move oddly, bobbing when they were in flat shielded water. A young drake dropped down and landed in the middle of the resting ducks.

The flock passed the landing area, and then it swung back around to make a final landing approach. The drake that had landed seemed to be fine. With cupped wings and exchanging a low chatter about what they were seeing, each duck used its body angle and tilt to weave its way down through the oncoming wind. At the last moment, with webbed feet forward, they hydroplaned to a splashy stop.

Many of the flock's members had already landed when three loud booms interrupted the white noise of the blowing wind. It was quickly followed by another three booms which intensified the panic through the flock. Two smoking sticks pointed out of an isolated patch of cane.

A drake flying just below Blossom had its wing fold backwards, and he spun bottom up and fell, hitting the water in an uncontrolled splash. She felt something pass through her right-wing feathers and three stings on her body. Her thick body feathers and down had shielded her enough from the steel pellets, stopping them before they penetrated her skin, but there would be bruising for sure. The flock instantly veered away from the sound, and she and her new mate pounded away with their wings, accelerating with the wind to put as much distance between them and the smoking sticks as possible. Though tired, they needed to move as far away as fast as they could.

Resting his gun stock against his leg, the hunter watched as his loyal friend swam back to the boat. "Good girl, Sam" the father said as the tan lab gently laid the second green head at his feet. He then gave Sam the signal to go again and retrieve the hen. His father's old Winchester Model 12 with its poly-choke had performed as well as the first day he went hunting with his dad and saw him skillfully use it.

His dad's memory was not his and Sam's only companion today. His fourteen-year-old son also now joined him in the family duck hunting legacy, using his grandad's old twenty-gauge pump Browning. The young man was still new to the sport, and his recognition of hens and drakes in flight was a work in progress, but it would come. Unlike the smaller teal and blue bills, these three mallards when dressed out would make heating up the oven a worthwhile investment. He cherished the thought of using his mom's old recipe for preparation and roasting them with bacon strips wrapped over the breasts.

Sam found the hen, turned, and paddled back toward the boat, waded over the sandbar, and lunged deftly aboard over the transom, reverently laying the soft brown hen next to the drakes. The hunter saw his son's face light up with a laugh as Sam vigorously shook her wet coat, sending a cold spray over everyone and everything in the boat.

Wiping their faces dry, they both picked up from the bottom of the narrow jon boat the spent shells, catching a faint residual odor of recently burnt propellant. Sam laid down on her spot at the bow, knowing she was appreciated and loved for doing her job well. The hunters inspected their guns to ensure they were empty, safeties on, and then secured them with the business ends pointing away from them and the dog. They untied and pushed the boat out of the blind they had made in fall using river cane and chicken wire that was mounted onto six heavy stakes driven into the soft sandy bottom. They slowly picked up their eighteen decoys. They wrapped the anchor cords around the bodies and slipped the circular anchors over the decoy heads, and then stowed them into the middle well of the boat.

Helped by the wind, they then drifted out of the blind and into deeper water. With his son's pull on its cord, the ten horsepower Mercury outboard revved to sputtering life, and they motored back to the boat launch, leaving the blind behind for another year. It had been a very successful last day of duck hunting season, especially considering that clear, crisp, windy days in late December normally favored the ducks.

Chapter 20
Remorse

The Christmas and New Year holidays had flown by, and upon returning to school, Helen made it a priority to pull out Randy Jackson's evaluations from when he was in her class the previous year. Before the break she had read his story on Mrs. Bishop's bulletin board, and then talked to Tina about it. She had needed to document the facts so that the bias or truthful error that was built into his prior year's record was removed and the accurate facts captured. This was part of her penitence, therapy, for having failed two sweet children.

She had decided that talking to Erma now that she was no longer at the school would not serve any purpose, knowing that she would be just as devastated as Helen to learn why Randy had acted the way he did. Indeed, she nor Erma were perfect, but they would still both regret having not questioned Randy with an open mind to find out why he did what he did. They had let the bias of his diagnosis blind them. She had also known that she needed to talk with Peggy about the revelation and her own failure.

Peggy had quietly listened as Helen uneasily explained what she had learned from Abigail. The principal smiled at Helen and said with an understanding look, "Try as we might, we are human, and only God is all knowing. Situations and information can slip past us, just like a snake in the grass. The demands on our minds and attention can block our view. We all should learn from this episode, but we must let it go." Helen looked down, wishing she could let it go.

Understanding Helen's humble mindset, Peggy continued. "You are no less of the caring and dedicated teacher you have always been because of this situation, and I know you will be a more perceptive teacher thanks to this experience. So do not beat yourself up. I know that is hard for you. Use it and continue to be the positive influence in your students' lives and the stable rock for your peers to confide in and rely on. Remember, we as a team did not catch it but as a team, we will address it and as best we can, use it to be better at what we do."

As she started to reread Randy's paperwork, Helen knew Peggy had been right.

She rationalized that Randy had only been in her class a few weeks before school had let out, so how could she have known him very well in such a brief period? She still felt she should have done better for him, but Peggy's words pushed her on.

Helen tried contacting Randy's parents by phone, but each time she was forced to leave a message. Several days later his mom left a voice message on her home phone during the school day that she did not need to talk about the situation. This frustrated Helen, as she wanted, needed, to express her remorse and explain what steps she had taken to expunge Randy's record of the negative content, and correctly record how he had shown compassion not harmful intent toward Danielle. It also left her concerned about his mom's true feelings for him and what his home life was really like.

Chapter 21
Starting Back

Blossom and her mate had chosen to winter in a Carolina rice plantation's irrigation canal, an area that was sought out by other large ducks. Being already paired up with a mature mate who weighed some 12 percent more than her, they were able to hold a spot in this roosting area and not be forced to use a less desirable one, like the younger ducks and unpaired females. Blossom was pleased to have found a mature and faithful defender.

The canal water level remained fairly constant. It had a small sandy beach below its high bank on the northwest side and a thick grove of trees at the base of the levy. The beach area was well-situated to catch the sun as it traveled on its path across the southern sky, providing a comfortable spot, where on sunny days they could rest in the late morning and early afternoon between trips to local agricultural fields to scavenge for rice, corn, soybeans, and alfalfa.

By mid-February, with longer days, the coldest of weather began to yield to the higher sun's warming effects. Soon they would gradually move north, along the Atlantic estuaries and coastal low country, as frozen lakes and streams opened, and the fields and ponds threw off their snow and ice blankets. Again, the large flocks would feel their collective internal compass leading them north to their breeding areas, and small groups would separate from the flock as they reached their individual home rivers and associated watershed wetlands.

By early March, they were back in the Barnegat Bay with thousands of other mallards, pintails, greater scaups, lesser scaups, blue bills, ring necks, goldeneyes, canvasbacks, redheads, mergansers, shovelers, blacks, and wood duck species, mixing about the wildlife preserve. Other species of lesser ducks plus cranes, terns, gulls, swans, geese, and herons all formed a swirling world of avian energy, grand and on the move, a natural epic movie full of hope and promise.

Chapter 22
Early Dismissal

Today's early dismissal was the right decision. It was one-thirty when the first large flakes began to fall, and the last buses pulled away from the loading zone. The snowfall was predicted to increase in intensity in an hour and last through the night. These late winter storms tended to produce a heavy wet snow that quickly turned roadways into frictionless surfaces, resulting in car spinouts everywhere. Many school districts had announced late starts for the following school day, and a few farther north in the more mountainous areas had already broadcast cancellations.

Helen had sent her birdfeeder crew out with instructions to put a little extra seed in the feeders in case the school day was canceled, which she expected would be the case if the forecast for ten to twelve inches of snow proved correct. That would mean an even shorter summer vacation, which had already been pushed back over a week to June twenty-fourth.

Today had been the one-hundredth school day of the year, which meant they were over halfway through the school year. In Helen's class they had marked the day by reading a book about some hungry ants that did things that totaled to one hundred. She also asked her students to share what they would want if they could have a hundred of something. Helen had almost lost her composure and teared a little when young Timothy said he would want a hundred hugs.

That morning, they had the main hundredth-day event, the parade of the first graders. All the other grades had lined up along the hallway outside their rooms to cheer them on as they marched by, wearing their hundredth-day vests made from paper bags. Each vest was uniquely decorated by its owner to illustrate something to do with the number one hundred. Some had a hundred pom-poms, stickers, or sequins; several had a ten-by-ten grid of many colors, or a math formula. The first graders had beamed as they made two trips around the square circuit of the school's main corridors.

Helen would not be staying late this afternoon, for she wanted to be home as soon as possible.

She had been petrified of driving in the snow ever since an incident she'd had back in high school. In another February snowstorm many years before, she had been driving her parent's station wagon to work at the Springfield Mall in northern Virginia, and traffic on I-95 North had been moving along well despite the building slush on the road. Temperatures, however, were below freezing, so when she headed across the Occoquan River bridge, the road surface changed to black ice. The bridge span sat over one hundred feet above the river below, and the station wagon started to slowly drift sideways. Helen frantically tried to stop the car and its slow spin, but nothing worked, and the car came to rest by hitting the guard rail on the north end of the bridge.

Behind her came other cars that were forced to change lanes, resulting in additional spinouts. Helen had been terrified she might go off the bridge or be hit by another car or worse, a tractor trailer. Fortunately, no severe damage was done to her or her family's car, but she still experienced long-term trauma from the incident and the mention of snow triggered the memory.

She now loved the all-wheel drive sedan her husband had bought her. More correctly, she loved that it handled well in the snow and would not leave her stranded at the bottom of their road that ran up the hill a quarter of a mile to her home. She still wished he had included her in picking out the car's color, but sometimes men have judgment lapses to put it kindly. 'Sometimes' actually was a lot more than kind.

When the last bus group was called, Helen gathered up student work she needed to assess, grabbed her purse and phone, and hit the road, hoping to be safely home before the roads were greased with slippery packed ice.

Chapter 23
New Home

Rivers flowed full as the snowmelt in New England churned away at riverbanks on their seasonal high flow trip to the ocean. Soon, with forests leafed out, the flows would drop as the growing trees and plants siphoned up any new rainfall, and the winter snow and ice melt surge would become a memory.

Blossom and her mate arrived at the confluence of the Housatonic and Naugatuck rivers in late March. Resting there a few days, the pair then departed one morning at dawn, flying up the Housatonic, taking their time to forage along the way in the flooded river backwaters and eddies. Eventually they arrived at the pond to find skim ice on its edges, and with little fanfare, the frozen trim around the pond quickly melted away once the sun rose above the tree line.

The trees were starting to bud, but still the forest was bare of leaves. Without the leaf canopy, the grasses and plants on the forest floor were greening up as the dark exposed ground readily absorbed the sun's energy. Canada geese had already arrived, and many were feeding on the tender skunk cabbage shoots that were just now poking up through the soft wet humus surrounding the vernal pools in the adjacent woods and wetlands.

Blossom and her mate departed the pond at midday to investigate the Marble Brook spa. Circling over the building, they saw that the parking lot was full of rumblers, and a recent heavy rain had left several spa pools on the roof. In the courtyard was a group of small two leggers, sitting on the concrete patio around the bench where a large two legger now rested. With the courtyard occupied, they decided now was not the time to explore it. Smaller two leggers were scattered around, chasing each other, and others were collected in small groups on the ball fields and asphalt playground.

Diverting away from their current circle pattern, the mallard couple traveled over the ridge to the nearby river, where several two leggers stood in the water with long sticks that had what looked to be spider filament shooting off the ends. They dropped down and flew over the two leggers, and then glided around the bend and landed in a sunny pool above a fast riffle. After doing a survey for predators, they paddled upstream against the current to a small shallow shoal of gravel, where they safely stood up out of the water and preened and oiled their feathers in the early morning light. Another great day at the beach. Their round trip of over fifteen hundred miles was complete, and Blossom's biological clock was telling her it was time to begin another cycle of new life.

As the sun settled down behind the trees, they stopped foraging on the river and flew back to Marble Brook. As expected, they found the parking lot almost deserted, and no two leggers were in sight. Circling silently without a quack or chortle around into the light warm breeze, they both cupped their wings and glided stealthily down to land in one of the roof's warm spa water pools. The water still held much of its daytime heat, which felt good on their webbed feet and legs.

Wading through the warm liquid, Blossom moved to the roof's edge and quickly peered over. The courtyard was clear, except for sparrows and finches at the bird feeders. The apple tree, being protected in the courtyard and from the heat radiating from the building, was already starting to sprout leaves and unfold its delicate white and pink blossoms. Descending into the yard, she paused to scan for any danger hidden in the shrubs or behind a tree. Thankfully, things were quiet, just as when she had left in the fall. Her mate soon followed, joining her on the ground.

They both took the opportunity to eat some of the scattered bird seed under the feeders, then dabbled down some water before moving to the western end of the yard to a deeper group of shrubs. Blossom sat down and began to pull leaves, twigs, and grass up close to her. Using her beak, she plucked some down feathers from her body and added them to the collection of nest grass and leaves underneath her.

In the morning, Blossom's mate having already fulfilled his husbandry role, said his goodbyes, and flew away to molt, leaving Blossom to nest and incubate her eggs. She would miss the comfort and protection of her strong mate, but that was the way of mallards.

Now alone, she deposited her first egg in the new nest. She would add another each day over the next twelve days, which collectively would be equivalent to half her body weight. The beauty of this place was that she could now leave the eggs, knowing they would be safe from all the traditional threats, and go wherever she felt for the day or night to forage and keep up her strength.

The days passed quickly, and the nightly pattern in the courtyard varied with sequence of classroom lights going on and off as the two legger pushed its noise maker through the building. This was followed by complete quiet, except for the static buzz and clicks of crickets and katydids. Their noise was not a real problem, though, as both bugs were tasty and high in protein, which her body needed as she produced eggs. During the day, Blossom would leave the nest and its growing clutch of eggs and then return each evening when things were quieter.

Her routine would change soon when she started to incubate

the eggs for four weeks. Then she would remain on the nest except to take short breaks for food and water. The good news was, both those needs could be satisfied within walking distance, plus the two leggers did not appear to know she and her nest existed. She liked her new home and the prospects it offered for success.

Chapter 24
Smartboard

Helen noted that the suet feeder on the apple tree was almost empty, and she would need to refill it. She contemplated doing it now, but she knew that was only a delay tactic to avoid having to figure out how to use the smartboard. The AV contractor had installed it over the weekend; supposedly, it was the latest and greatest innovation that would open a whole universe of multi-media teaching tools at her fingertips. For her, though, it was the great unknown. What she did know, and truthfully feared, was that her students probably knew more about how to use it than she did.

Overhead projectors and chalkboards she understood, and she had prepared materials using those tools to teach the curriculum. She was still trying to understand the software they used on their school computers, and now they wanted her to use this screen in conjunction with her classroom computer to teach. She would have to rebuild most of her instructional teaching aids on the computer just to display them on the smartboard.

Sitting down at her computer, she took out her training notes that Brianna had provided the prior week, having decided she must try to put aside her fear and try. "Let me Google the video for the song 'Africa' and see if it will play on my computer," she said to the empty room, as she peered into the screen and toggled to the search engine. "Got it," she exclaimed, and entered the Vevo site and watched the obligatory ad. "Enough of that," she decided, clicking her mouse on the "skip ad" button. The song's steady beat began, and she started to move with it, letting the song wash away some of her angst. Now that she had the song on her computer, she needed to share it with the smartboard. Nothing. Try again. Nothing. She growled along with the wild dogs crying out in the night in Africa. "Buggers!" she cried, slamming her mouse on her desk.

"Are you alright, Helen?" came a sweet voice from her doorway. It was Judy, one of the new third grade teachers. Helen took a deep breath and explained how she was just trying to figure out how to get her computer to show on the smartboard. "Maybe I can help?" Judy offered. She picked up a small controller sitting on the corner of Helen's desk and pushed a button. Immediately the smartboard came to life, its sound system starting to blast at full volume. Helen flushed and dropped her head into her hands.

Chapter 25
The Wait

Blossom sat on thirteen eggs, which she had started to incubate. If she lost an egg at this point, it would not be replaced this season. She would leave the nest for two short periods each day to eat and drink water, but the rest of the time she would keep her body and its warmth sitting on her new brood's eggs. Her recent routine had been to slip away before the big yellow rumblers arrived in the morning, and then return to the courtyard as the sun set each night. What occurred in the courtyard each day was unknown, but she hoped and needed to stay undetected for the next four weeks. Like every mother duck, her lack of mobility during this period would present several hazards to her and the eggs.

The priority was to keep the eggs warm. Periodically, she would turn and move each egg to uniformly distribute her warmth. Weather was always a factor, as it was not unheard of to have cold weather in April, and even sleet and snow. On the other end of the spectrum, especially as weather warmed, violent storms with high winds, heavy rain, and hail were to be expected. The nest site she had selected was on higher ground, next to the building, which would hopefully keep her nest dry even when water ponded up during long or heavy periods of rain. Tucked deep beneath the shrubs, she had the benefit of their limbs and leaves deflecting anything liquid or frozen from impacting her or the nest. As if thinking about it was the cause, a cold rain began to apply a wet sheen on all the courtyard surfaces and walkways. With a couple of chirps, a pair of cardinals departed the feeders and headed out of the courtyard to their own place of shelter.

The cold rain, never hard, lasted two days, and the courtyard remained free of two leggers. The second night, a chilly breeze started to push the clouds out, but not before a light snow fell and stuck on all the surfaces that were above the ground and on top of the grass. Blossom fluffed her feathers to insulate the eggs from the freezing air and keep them dry. She did not leave to eat as normal, to ensure the embryos were not exposed to the cold conditions.

The rain kept all the two leggers indoors. Most mornings, though, two or three of them did still go to the bird feeders and fill them. On rainy days at the same time in the morning, she would hear a window groan open and several swishes as seed was thrown out the window and hit the ground. This was always good to hear, as she would not have to hunt for the miniscule amount the songbirds scattered from the platform feeders' trays. She really needed to eat, since she had skipped a couple of meals to ensure the eggs stayed warm during the recent cold snap. The question was, when would be the best time to leave the nest to do so?

She decided to wait till later in the day, when the sun still warmed the courtyard, the big yellow rumblers had departed with their little two leggers, and the building had settled into its late afternoon and nighttime peacefulness.

For nine days, the yellow rumblers stayed away, and the courtyard and building remained quiet and mostly deserted. The recent chill was gone, and things were warming up nicely each day.

The longer daylight hours appeared to spur tree branch buds to explode with tender new green leaves. The apple tree blossoms now fell to the ground, creating a sense of enchantment around its base. Bees continued to hum around the remaining blooms, collecting their residual pollen, and white butterflies with black tipped wings now fluttered through the yard several times a day. The only problem was that no two leggers were coming to fill the feeders and by the third day, she was having to hunt around the courtyard to find food.

Finally, the yellow rumblers and two leggers returned, and the building took in a deep breath of energy. The warmer weather necessitated the windows be opened. Blossom could hear the sounds from the rooms around the courtyard, hearing but not understanding the squawk of the speaker system, the shuffle of desks and chairs, cabinet doors opening and closing, the smartboards playing videos, and the ever-present sounds of students talking, laughing, and squealing, increasing and decreasing in their decibel levels, punctuated by the teachers' commanding voices as they tried to keep their young charges focused on learning when ball season and the outdoors beckoned.

Two-legger appearances in the courtyard increased. In addition to the feeder crew, on bright, sunny days, groups of about twenty would come into the courtyard and gather around the bench seat. Fortunately, none of them wandered close to her shrubs and nest, but she kept alert in case one strayed too close. When they were present, she stayed perfectly still, not wanting any movement to attract any unwanted eyes and attention.

She recognized the machine as soon as she saw it. She was surprised because the big yellow rumblers had left, and she did not expect to have company at that time in the late afternoon. A very big two legger was pushing the horizontal noise machine that chewed off the grass. It started roaring next to the doors on the west side of the building as the two legger pushed it around and under the shrubs on that side of the yard, slinging grass, twigs, and leaves in a cloud of dust and dirt into the air. It seemed to be systematically working its way around the area, attacking each shrub and tree planted on the perimeter of the yard, then moving back and forth in a straight line over larger patches of grass. All the while grinding away on the grass stems, leaving everything at an even height.

Soon the roaring machine approached her group of shrubs. The noise was deafening, and the dust made her choke. Blossom was terrified as it moved past her to the left of the shrub in front of her, and then retreated to make another charge, which collided with the same shrub and rained down twigs and dead leaves from the impact it made into the shrub's trunk. It hesitated and retreated again, and then made another charge directly at her. She could see leaves and stems being shredded under its mean spitting breath. She automatically squinted to keep the growing cloud of debris from blowing into her eyes. Her body vibrated, along with the eggs underneath her, as the machine continued to race toward her. As it touched her fluffed up breast feathers, its left side caught a low branch and stopped, but then it sprung forward enough to suck away some of the down lining the nest's edge. Her head, nest, and breast feathers rippled with the surging air around the machine. It retreated again before charging once more, this time, on the other side of the next shrub. Blossom's heart was pounding. Seized with fear, she fought an overwhelming urge to flee, but she willed herself to stay still and not reveal her presence and the precious treasure in her nest.

The machine moved methodically and slowly away from her. Her emotions were overwhelmed with a combination of fear and relief, and her body quivered uncontrollably. She hoped to never be that close again to a two legger and their noise makers. She needed to wash her beak to rid it of the gritty debris thrown all over her and the nest, but she was afraid to move. Finally, the noise stopped. Rising slowly, Blossom fluffed and rearranged her feathers, shaking dust and debris off her, forming a small dust cloud under the shrubs. Once she had cleared her feathers and the air, she repositioned all the eggs and settled back down to try and subdue her traumatized state of being. Her eggs would never understand or appreciate her courage and heroism in the face of nearly becoming part of a big duck egg omelet.

Chapter 26
A Surprise

The month of May as well as the school year was mostly in the rear-view mirror. The kindergarteners had their Halloween costume parade back in October, with comic characters like Spiderman, Batman, Captain America, and Wonder Woman all being well represented, along with the perennial Disney Cinderella and more recent royalty Anna, Elsa, and their friend Olaf. The Johnson twins really were the cutest in their lightning bug costumes—a black jacket and long coat tails with a yellow sack underneath and a flashing strobe light—and their cute, giggling smiles as their springy antennas with Styrofoam ball ends danced about on their black beany caps.

November got rolling with Veterans Day, with local veterans visiting and students telling stories about veterans in their families, including Helen sharing about her grandfather who had fought at the beaches of Normandy, the Battle of the Bulge, and in Korea. He had also served in Vietnam with his son, her dad, who later became a three-star general in the Marine Corps. She understood the sacrifices that parents and families who had loved ones in the service made.

Thanksgiving had flown by and Christmas had brought about a lot of celebrations, and the gingerbread smell had permeated the school as the first graders made candy decorated houses for display. Gingerbread had made its curtain call in January, when the kindergarteners had a school-wide search for the gingerbread man, who had miraculously appeared in the cafeteria oven cornered by the schools' cooks. As was always expected that time of year, they had experienced a string of school opening delays and early dismissals as snow and ice made their seasonal impact on every activity and plan.

In February the valentine cards had been made for moms and dads plus the first graders morphed into leprechauns, searching the school to find their pot of gold.

April had seen the start of outside sports programs plus Easter egg artwork was displayed on bulletin boards and the spring break school holiday had allowed a few families to visit Disney World in Florida.

The classroom moms had been very easy to work with this year, and they had planned fun and creative celebrations for the second-grade class, despite it being the nut-free group. They would help again this afternoon with the class author celebration, where the students would share their compositions with classmates and family. The class would separate into small groups and meet at designated points around the school, including outside at the bench in the courtyard, if the weather permitted.

Helen noted that Connie and Joshua had come back in and were putting away the seed pail and scoop. She casually drifted over to the windows to check their work at the feeder; they had been replenished properly. It appeared she would need to fill one of the suet holders soon, though. As she started to look away, some movement near the holly bush caught her eye. Looking down, she found herself looking eye to eye with the cocked head of a brown colored duck with a black and dark orange beak.

"A duck!" she inadvertently said out loud. All the little eyes immediately looked up at her. Seeing the direction in which she was looking, several students bolted to the window, and one announced, "Babies!" Helen watched as one after another, thirteen yellow and brown puffs of peeping fuzz appeared around their mom, some already pecking at the scattered seed on the ground. One was floating confidently in the water pan. The class's attention to their work was understandably lost, so she told the students to slowly come to the window to see the new arrivals.

Blossom could see the two legger with beautiful gold-like feathers on its head looking directly at her. Its eyes were beautiful and kind, not threatening, and she appeared to welcome a bond. Next to it were smaller sets of wide eyes, staring back at her through the open windows. She was not sure what to do as her ducklings scrambled around her. She decided it best she move on out of sight along the wall and keep her and her babies under the cover of the bushes where possible.

Suddenly, Helen realized it was about eleven forty-five a.m., lunch time for her class, and they needed to get moving quickly, as they were late. "Melissa, please form the lunch line at the door," Helen commanded. The girl did not respond, and no one was moving toward the exit. Gently touching her shoulder, she softly pleaded, "Melissa, please form the lunch line at the door." Melissa reluctantly turned, and then Helen gently scooched the kids away from the window and toward the door. The class energy was off the chart, as each one could not wait to share what they had seen. Finally, with everyone in line and segregated by meal choice, with those who brought their lunch at the line's end, the class marched single file next to Helen to the cafeteria, arriving three minutes behind schedule.

The students got in their respective serving station lines to obtain their food, and when served, joined those who brought lunches at the two tables assigned to their class. Along the way, Mrs. Dean's students were sharing the news. As Olga the hot meal server handed Bridgette her plate, the little girl proudly explained that her class had a duck and ducklings. Olga never ceased to be amazed at the imagination of children, knowing pets were not allowed in the school due to allergies. There had been, however, one recent exception, as one of the characters in the *Trumpet of the Swan* book for the One School-One Read program was a red slider turtle, and someone had donated an adult red slider to the school, along with an aquarium to house it. The turtle, named Marbles, now lived in the school lobby.

As Albert walked toward his table with his nachos, he saw his older sister on the other side of the cafeteria, and he yelled, "Sis! There is a mother duck and ducklings in the courtyard!"

"Quiet, no yelling!" the teacher intern on cafeteria duty said sternly. Not that it was going to be a secret, but Albert's announcement spread the news faster than a forest fire in the dry West. Containing and controlling it now would not be possible.

That afternoon teachers in all the classrooms bordering the courtyard were having to constantly pull their students away from the windows and back to their desks. The consensus seemed to be that there were a hen and thirteen ducklings now making their home at Marble Brook.

Chapter 27
Memorial Day Holiday

The courtyard was brightened by the lights in Helen's class the Saturday evening of the Memorial Day long weekend. Helen was afraid that the ducklings might starve over the extended weekend break. Her husband James was pretty sure a wild duck could take care of itself and its family without human intervention, but there was no convincing Helen, who wanted to install a larger pan of water for the ducklings to swim in and drink. The larger and deeper pan, however, made it difficult for the short legged little blessings to make it up into the new water feature.

Having been out of town on business most of the week, his idea of a Saturday night date had not really been to carry a piece of bluestone, a large metal pan, along with several large buckets of water, into a half-lit courtyard at nine p.m. He worked to make an indention in the soil to stabilize the pan, then rested a flat piece of bluestone on a small piece of wood, such that the squared edge matched the level of its top edge. He placed a wedge shaped piece of stone inside of the water pan so that the ducklings could easily climb back out of it.

Blossom and the ducklings had been under the apple tree when the room lights had come on. Upon hearing the courtyard door latch clank as the large two leggers entered, she had quickly scurried toward the nearest dark corner, her ducklings in tow, as she wanted to move them to the other side, away from the lights and intruders. When Helen went back inside and her husband exited the courtyard, Blossom immediately moved her family diagonally across the yard to the denser shrubs and nest area at the far end. Soon after, the two leggers returned, each carrying a container, which after the contents were dumped, she discovered were water and seed, so they would not starve or die of thirst. "Ok, are we done?" James asked. "Yes, I think they should be good for now. Thanks for coming and helping me," Helen said, smiling, and giving him a quick peck on the lips.

At first light, Blossom and her ducklings traveled around the perimeter to reach the newly provisioned feeding area and enlarged pool facility. The ducklings immediately took to the water feature, splashing and paddling, tumbling up and down the ramps. Along with Blossom, they also ate their fill of the seed that now was in small piles underneath the apple tree.

Chapter 28
Missing

Not since the One School-One Read announcement had the school seemed to have so much energy. The courtyard became off limits to unauthorized persons to keep little eyes and hands from disturbing its new residents. There was unfettered joy and excitement at Marble Brook.

Helen went to school early the Wednesday morning after Memorial Day so that she could make some photocopies before other teachers arrived and created a waiting line. Curious too, she took a glance out the window to see if the ducks were there. Indeed, they were. Blossom looked up when Helen appeared in the window. Helen saw the ducklings spread between the seed piles and the water pan, all in constant motion. She counted them several times but with all the movement, she was not sure of the count. It appeared that there were only twelve not thirteen ducklings. From her view through the window, though, the thirteenth could easily be under the holly bush or up right against the building out of her line of sight.

Later in the day a sighting was reported, also of only twelve ducklings. Perhaps someone needed to go into the courtyard, despite it being off limits, to see if there was a lost duckling.

The buses had just departed on Thursday morning, when a streak of air-to-ground lightning strobed the classroom windows with blinding light and a distinctive explosive crackling sound that startled everyone. It was followed by earth and desk shaking thunder that trembled through the school, making pencils bounce and the window glass rattle in its frame. Another blast came almost immediately, and then large raindrops splattered long streaks at a downward angle on the windows, and visibility outside dropped to only a few feet as a rain column squeezed out its heavy torrent of water. Some of the kindergarteners were scared by the storm's noise and light show, while other students were plastered up next to the windows to see nature's fireworks.

In the ensuing downpour the ducks moved quickly away from the bird feeders, heading for the shrubs. The mother duck was in the lead, but only eleven ducklings were following her. Where were the other two? Did they run off and become separated when the lightning struck the nearby woods, or had they already been gone before the storm? Speculation and rumors were starting to spread about the missing ducklings. Did they die? Were they trapped? Was there a rat in the courtyard? Perhaps a cat had somehow managed to get in. The concerns and calls for some sort of action were bubbling up, and the school nurse observed that students having emotional episodes increasing.

Friday morning, a report came in that the duckling count was down to ten. What was happening to them? At nine-forty-five the cause revealed itself. Patty Williams' classroom was located on the north side of the courtyard, and it faced one of two larger trees that grew there. She, like everyone now in the school, would periodically look outside to see if she could spot the ducks.

Sitting midway down the largest tree that faced her classroom windows, on a branch that overhung the walkway, sat a large sharp-shinned hawk. It is a beautiful bird, with distinctive head markings, soft brindled burnt orange breast feathers and checkered black and white wings. Patty knew why it was there, and it was not good. Not good at all.

Chapter 29
The Stand Off

Nails felt proud that she was the first hawk that had the good luck to spot them. This was not a traditional place for her to hunt for food to feed her young eyases. It had been a late afternoon when she had glided low across the grass that bordered the ball fields in the hopes of finding a mouse, small rabbit, or vole venturing out to munch on some tender new growth grass. Having come up empty, she had sailed up and over the school and was about to make a return trip along the ball fields, when she had spotted the tiny ducks in the shadowy area under the apple tree. She had made a last-minute change for her evening's menu, opting for some nice tender spring duckling.

Circling back, she had landed in the top of the tallest courtyard tree. Blossom had seen Nails land and immediately sounded the alarm, the ducklings crowding up next to her as she had tried to quickly move them all up under the holly tree as best as she could. Nails had eyed the little family and couldn't believe her luck to have so many options. She had bowed her neck and given a long heart stopping screech that had shot through the little ducks' emotional engines, and three of them that could not fit under

Blossom's right wing had bolted from her in different directions. *Too easy*, Nails had thought, as she then launched down and effortlessly closed her left talons around the one that had headed toward the far side of the yard. There were no trash talking ducklings that day, as her talons clinched the terrified evening meal.

Nail's strategy had worked the same way for the next two days. She had circled high overhead, awaiting the little duck family to reveal itself. When she had identified her targets, she dropped down to land on the tree nearest to her prey, announcing her presence with her loud piercing screech to unnerve the young waterfowl who were trapped inside the four walls of the courtyard. Each day, at least one duckling had been betrayed by their feet when they had run away from the threatening sound. That movement was all Nails had needed to finish her mission and feed her family.

Nails once again sat in one of the trees, the ducks caught under a small shrub between two larger ones. When they bolted, Nails would have a clear shot at them on either side. "Sre-e-e-e-ch!" her lungs launched her menacing call toward the hiding place, but no ducklings appeared. *Do they really think I am just going to sit by and let them hide?* Just as she was about to sling another scream of terror at the ducks, a door latch clanked loudly, and a large two legger carrying a broom bolted into the yard, its eyes immediately locking with Nails'.

What do we have here? Nails wondered. *I have seen these before in passing, but how rude to interrupt my shopping trip. What gives them the right to stand between me and the food for my family? What does 'Shoo, shoo, shoo mean?' It keeps barking it over and over and over, thrashing the poor tree limbs with the broom. What has this tree done to it to make it throw such a fit and beat it so? Surely it cannot be about me. I have never attacked a two legger in my life, so why all the theatrics? Maybe this is its nesting tree, and it does not want me sitting in it. Ok then, I will move over to that tree, which is not ideal but still gives me an angle to the ducklings.*

Just as Nails sprang from the limb, Blossom, who had been watching this all play out, seized the opportunity to move her and the ducklings to the larger patch of shrubs. Distracted by the wild two legger, Nails saw the ducks move and she tried to make a quick adjustment to cut them off. She could catch one but almost too late, she realized that the broom was no longer held by the two legger, and it was spinning directly at her and closing fast, forcing her to veer to avoid a certain impact and injury. No sooner than the broom hit the ground, the two legger picked it up and was charging at her again, appearing ready to launch another attack.

"My oh my, what terrible tempers those two leggers have. They are nastier than a one-legged rooster. They have absolutely no measure of respect for the rights and needs of other citizens of the world. What is the world coming to?" she muttered, deciding that a small duck was not worth the risk of injury, then flying quickly up and out of sight of the courtyard and its crazy two legger. "The ducks might think I am bad but watch out for the squawking two legger my feathered friends, beware!"

Chapter 30
The Removal

Patty Williams' confrontation with the prime suspect responsible for the recent duckling abductions was seen by several observers, some of whom cheered when she launched the broom at the attacker. She and the rest of the staff had a lot of other work they needed to complete before the school year ended, though, and constantly defending the mallard family was not going to be feasible. Teachers with classrooms bordering the courtyard were also having to move students away from the windows and back to their work, which was impacting their learning process.

Chief Betty had a lot to do, as in her role she handled most of the tactical everyday questions that came into the school office, coordinated the staff necessities, and supported Peggy. Despite the pressing year-end needs, she recognized that a sustainable strategy was required to protect the ducks. She suggested to Principal Booker that she thought the best course of action was to move the ducklings to an environment where they had a fighting chance to survive. At the present time, in the truest meaning of the phrase, they were sitting ducks. "Let the custodians know that we want the duck family safely removed from the courtyard," Peggy said. "Today, if at all possible, so we can focus on wrapping up the school year and keep students engaged in their work." Betty looked at the clock, realizing that the head custodian would have already left for the day, so she would need to talk with the evening custodian.

"It's simple," she said to Ed, the custodian. "Just corner and capture them, then take them to a nearby pond." Ed expressed with his hands as if someone was standing next to him. Oh, it was simple all right. Simple as playing tennis. The problem in this match was that he was faced with an opponent that could literally fly around the courtyard like Federer or Nadal. He was already soaked with sweat and sat down on the stone bench to catch his breath, regroup, and figure out a new strategy. Momma duck was not going to forfeit the match. He on the other hand was considering it.

He found a YouTube video that showed a mother duck with her ducklings, parading down the school hallway from a school courtyard to the outside of the building. The mother duck, who apparently had been undetected, had pecked on the door to be let out through the school hallway. His duck was not wanting to go anywhere near a door.

Another video with the same trapped duckling situation showed a custodian with a yellow tennis ball stuck on the end of a broom handle, pushing the ball on the floor next to the mother duck and ducklings along a hallway, the ducks following along. He wondered out loud, "How do you train ducks to follow a ball? Does the mother think it is an escaping egg and wants to incubate it, and the ducklings just follow her?"

Not thinking either of these videos were a viable solution for the situation at Marble Brook, he looked at another video, which showed a man using a large piece of cardboard to move the mother duck and ducklings toward the open door to a hallway leading to the outside of the building. The problem was the mother duck would not go through the doorway. She kept running from one side of the door to the other, but she refused to go in. When the man got too close to the mom, she would abandon her three ducklings and fly to another part of the courtyard.

This momma duck seemed to be conflicted, as apparently six other ducklings had fallen into a drain in the middle of the courtyard, and a duckling hero climbed down into the storm drain and retrieved them, and they happily rejoined their other three siblings. Now the man focused on corralling the nine ducklings into the doorway. Momma flew out of the courtyard and landed on top of the school. He pressed on with the ducklings through the school hallway and to an outside door.

The momma duck, finally hearing them outside the school, was peering over the edge of the roof. When the ducklings moved far enough away from the people, she rejoined them, leading them to a nearby pond.

The video's duck, Ed thought, must be a close relative of his momma duck. He headed to the school truck loading dock looking for what he needed. He found a piece of corrugated sheet that had been wrapped around a file cabinet that had just been delivered, and he proceeded back toward the courtyard. He needed this to work soon before it got too dark for man or duckling, as there was no courtyard lighting other than what spilled out through the windows of a lit classroom.

Ed closed the hallway fire doors on both sides of the breezeway corridor, having opened and pinned the outside entrance door open to the playground. He then proceeded to do the same for the courtyard entrance door. With the passage now open and interior hallways blocked off, his strategy was to try and move the ducklings toward the courtyard entrance door.

The momma duck did not seem happy, initially choosing the fight not flight reflex, throwing herself at him with violently flapping wings such that he had to duck, no pun intended, to avoid impact. A long series of distressed quacks followed as he stayed focused on the peeping little ones. A couple of the little guys kept breaking away from the main group and going behind the bushes, where he could not easily block them with his board. Like the last video he had viewed, they did not sense or accept that there was a way out. Finally, he was able to bend the corrugated barrier around them in a semi-circle and push the ducklings into the doorway. Gently, he moved the corrugated barrier up against them, driving them up onto the door threshold. Several bounced off the step and rolled backwards but regained their feet quickly, successfully jumping to the higher level on the second try. They then reluctantly moved down the corridor heading toward the outside door. Without their momma in sight, the stressed peeping was even more sorrowful. Ed tried to move them gingerly toward the outside entrance, but his little band of refugees heard their mother quacking in the doorway behind him, and he was leading them in the other direction.

As he got the ducklings to the outside doorway landing, he decided to back away and return into the middle of the corridor, where he stepped quickly through a fire door and into the interior hallway, and out of the momma duck's sight. He kept the doorway slightly open, however, to allow him to still see if the ducklings would retreat. Thankfully, Momma, seeing a clear shot to her ducklings, bravely flew through the courtyard doorway and down the corridor to her babies. Ed stepped back into the corridor with his board and pressed Momma to continue with her ducklings out the entrance to the asphalt playground and on toward the ball fields.

Knowing that the hawks and other predators would still be active, Ed pulled the school entrance closed and locked it, and then continued to herd Momma and the string of ducklings across the open playground to the gap that led to the beaver pond. He observed the family was less stressed now, as the quacking and peeping had quieted to a low chatter, and it was much less frantic in tone. At the pace of little running web feet, they moved steadily across over seventy-five yards of open field to an opening in the fence line. Once there, the refugees hit the pathway to the nearby beaver pond.

Seeing them move into the water, Ed headed back to the school building. He still had to finish his night's work. Duck wrangling had cost him almost two hours, and he still needed to vacuum every room, collect, and then take out the trash, wipe down cafeteria tables, clean bathrooms, and more. Still, he had prevailed; set, game, match. He could hear the crowd roar at his triumph.

Chapter 31
Duck Update

The next morning, Principal Booker checked with Betty on the status of the ducks. She hoped that the momma duck and her ducklings had successfully and safely been removed. Betty reported that Ed had left a note on her desk indicating that they indeed were successfully relocated to the nearby beaver pond. Peggy informed all the teachers with classrooms facing the courtyard.

Meanwhile, Helen checked her mail slot and found an invitation to a baby shower for Monica, a member of her second-grade team, who was expecting. Being the team leader, she would need to line up a substitute teacher while Monica was on maternity leave. She was thrilled for Monica. She and her husband had been trying to start a family for some time, unsuccessfully, and they had begun looking to adopt. Their prayer for a miracle had happened, and they were now looking forward to having twins. Helen had raised three children, and she knew how one baby could strip you of rest and energy. With two babies at the same time, she prayed that God would give Monica and Bill strength to weather the challenge those bundles of joy would present. Helen suspected that

Monica may not be coming back to teach, as she could tell that she was a nurturer. "We'll see," she said to herself.

As she was heading out of the office, Betty said, "Helen, if you have not already heard, the ducks have been moved to the pond. Ed did it last night." "Thanks for letting me know. Glad we don't have to watch them disappear one at a time," Helen responded. Smiling, she left the office. She would have to let her bird feeder crew know that they no longer needed to throw seed on the ground for the ducks. They would be missed, but everyone would be glad they were in a better place where they could survive and escape the preying hawks.

As Helen turned into the hallway, she almost head-butted Annie Dixon, whose daughter Fenley she had taught two years prior. "Excuse me for not looking where I was going," Helen said, catching Annie by the arm to avoid falling over. "No problem, Mrs. Dean," the woman replied. "Fenley says you are still her favorite teacher." "What a sweetheart," Helen replied. Fenley was Annie's oldest and indeed a bright and well-mannered young girl, who had been a pleasure to teach. She had two younger siblings, both boys. "I have requested that Stevie be in your class next year," Annie said hopefully. Helen smiled and squeezed her hand. It was a sweet thing to hear. Helen knew there had been talk of cutting a second-grade class if the school budget, which had failed voter approval once, failed again at the next vote. "It would be great to have another Dixon in my class next year. Hopefully the budget will pass this time so that we can finalize the number of classes and placements. Good to have bumped into you and tell Fenley I say hi," Helen said. "I need to get going to my class. You have a great day, Annie." It was always nice to have a parent reaffirm the positive impact you had on their child. That said, she already knew that Stevie was a handful and was very different from his sister.

Stevie was exactly the type of student she was there for, hopefully to make a difference in their life. It was always amazing how different children could be despite having the same parents and home to grow up in. Her husband's theory was that God made each child different so that no matter the circumstances, one offspring would find success and help the family. "Hi, Mrs. Dean," said Jack another former student, as he sped down the hall to class. Helen grinned and almost teared up, remembering how he had always expressed his appreciation for her when in class.

Chapter 32
The Pond

Blossom was relieved to be back at the pond with her ten ducklings. The last few days had been intense. Now she was in an environment she knew and where the water provided a barrier and a means for escape, which the ducklings were uniquely designed to utilize. That said, she also knew well that despite the benefits the pond provided, there were still all the dangers she had before. Rusty, Knees, Legs, Chomps, Snuggles, Rat Snake, Nails, and Eyeballs were all willing to welcome her little paddlers sooner or later with open mouths.

The ducklings were enjoying the pond and its deeper water and wider expanse. Already diving and popping back to the surface, they naturally adapted to their second home and were exploring the new things found in the water and on the banks that did not exist in the courtyard. Frogs were a very curious creature, along with their wiggling offspring, and lots and lots of new bugs full of concentrated protein needed by ducklings to grow up fast.

As darkness crept in, the new night sounds were scary for the ducklings in contrast to the isolated quiet of the courtyard after the long-nosed noise maker went silent. There was the hum of mosquitoes, flying beetles with flashing yellow firefly lights, the screeching of katydids, crickets, and mating calls of tree frogs, joined by the deep croaking of their bullfrog cousins, providing a full range of nature's harmony and rhythm. Later, as the evening chorus faded, they heard the haunting "Hoo, hoo, hoooo" calls of a pair of barred owls, drifting through the dark moon shadowed woodlands. These nocturnal raptors, with their quiet flight, stealth, and night vision, presented a unique threat, especially if you were a small rodent running around in the soft blue hues or an errant duckling thinking a nighttime swim was a fun idea.

Blossom reflected on her nesting paradise as her little ones nestled up against her for warmth in the damp night air. The courtyard had been a perfect place until the horizontal noise maker showed up and came so close to having destroyed her and the eggs. The thought sent a shudder through her body again which caused the ducklings to reposition themselves up against her. She had seen where the noise maker went and if she relocated her nest a little deeper, it would be safe, she thought. She could handle its noise given a little more space.

For the most part, the two leggers otherwise had not attacked them until today. There was more seed on the ground after she had seen the big two legger with the fine golden feathers on its head through the window. It had understanding eyes plus all its little ones had curious expressions. She had recognized some of those smaller two leggers bringing the seed out to the apple tree and pouring it on the ground, which was not the case before, when the seed had only been put in the feeders. It was like they wanted them to stay. Then there was a larger puddle of water near the seed that had the ramps for the ducklings. It was put there one night by the shiny headed one and the other one with golden head feathers.

Then there was the two-legger sorcerer with its broom who had tried to put the spell on Nails. The sorcerer spoke to some spirit with its loud incantation of "Shoo, shoo, shoo," repeating the spell, and then the broom levitated toward Nails barely missing the raptor. This act allowed Blossom's family to successfully retreat to the safety of the denser shrub shelter. Immediately, the sorcerer began chanting a new spell. Nails, fearing for her life and suspecting she might not avoid the levitated broom a second time, decided to fly away. The two-legger sorcerer had been their savior.

Then there was the big, dark, short-feathered two legger today, who at first was chasing her around the courtyard, trying to corner and catch her with its large stubby claws. It just kept coming at her, no matter where she went. Eventually, it quit the pursuit and rested on the bench before disappearing through the closed doors for a while. The doors had opened with a familiar clank and stayed opened. Instead of going after her, the two legger started going after her babies with that big piece of material. Going after her was one thing but going after her babies was just cowardly and wrong. *I barely missed giving that bully a piece of my forewing to think about.*

But was it really attacking my ducklings? No, she finally surmised. *It was more like it was trying to get us to go through the opening, a tunnel to the outside.* Did it trap them? No, it had moved them slowly and gently to the outside of the building toward the open field, and then left them there and got out of her way.

In the excitement and fear, she had not recognized what it was trying to do. Now she realized it was trying to help her ducklings escape from the courtyard and Nails. *Oh my, how embarrassing. It must think I am a terrible, ungrateful, and stupid momma duck.* She had tried to deck the two legger and despite the assault, it had still helped them get outside and to the pond. She really must be suffering from PEHD (Post Egg Hatching Depression) or something to not understand what it was trying to do, free them from the courtyard. This was a special two legger indeed.

Yes, the two leggers in paradise had only tried to help in their individual ways, and she had been too blinded by fear to understand. *Next year I think I will go back again, and maybe I will be less fearful of them and look past their quirkiness and allow them to help. Perhaps we can be closer friends despite my ungrateful actions, I hope.*

Thankful for and relieved by her epiphany about the two leggers, Blossom rested with one eye open, just in case someone was watching. She snoozed with her ducklings, contented and at peace with her new world reality and its options and with a newfound appreciation for the two-leggers.

Chapter 33
A Crowd

Blossom adjusted quickly to her old pond environment. She had to; in her absence there had appeared some new residents. First, she spotted Petals, who now had five ducklings of her own, then a Canada goose Thelma and her mate Bernard, with their four goslings, who were already foraging the pond for food. Adding her own ten ducklings, their shared world was becoming crowded, and the supply of underwater plants, tadpoles, bugs, water plants, and minnows would soon be exhausted. Petals, having faced the nesting threats and failed to protect most of her eggs, was both delighted but amazed to see her mother with ten ducklings, twice the number she had. *How had she done that?* Petals wondered.

The goslings, with their longer necks, could reach more of the bottom of the pond and higher up on surrounding plants. That, coupled with their large appetites, was creating a growing challenge for all the ducklings as each day passed. No longer could they just dabble in the shallows or pick off bugs on the low vegetation. Now they had to dive to reach any of the underwater food or move farther away from the water to find bugs and tender vegetation. The plentiful grain supply in the courtyard was history, and the pond had a limited amount of nourishing biomass.

This situation was far from dire for Cuddles and Chomps. The increased waterfowl population, probing ever deeper into the water for a meal, presented many more opportunities to eat. And eat they did. As one might expect, a gosling was the first to disappear, becoming a banquet for Chomps, Cuddles, their year-old snapping turtle youngsters, and other permanent pond residents, including crayfish and minnows. Nothing would be wasted as nature moved all its members toward a new equilibrium.

By late spring, the waterfowl population had already shrunk by six, including two of Blossom's current offspring. Rusty had nabbed one of Petals' ducklings, who had strayed in pursuit of a large mayfly too close to a patch of grass where he was concealed. The fact that Blossom and her remaining brood had to risk increased exposure to all predators to find food was a daily concern and consequence of her successfully hatching all thirteen of her eggs.

In early summer, with her brood now flying, Blossom often moved to a small river nearby to find enough food to allow the ducklings' bodies to grow and build up fat reserves. She and Petals too needed to rebuild their own strength and energy reserves that had been depleted during the breeding season, which was a requirement if they were to survive the migration and winter's challenges. There Blossom found wood ducks and mergansers, already foraging with their own ducklings. Fortunately, she had spied a nearby farmer's cornfield that had recently been harvested and tilled. There were scattered kernels to be found mixed in the rows of soil, along with high protein cornsilk caterpillars, grubs, and worms. Fortunately, the different duck species had different food preferences, mergansers liking fish, wood ducks preferring berries and acorns, while Blossom and her crew were omnivores, eating insects, invertebrates, plants, snails, and plant seeds. There was no food shortage in the neighboring areas surrounding the pond.

Some nights they would return to the pond to rest, but they had increasingly frequented an overgrown island sandbar above one of the dams on the river. The isolation of the sandbar provided a haven at all hours of the day. When disturbed, they could easily paddle upstream or fly over the dam and downstream to where the river ran into a large lake.

Eventually, they started to meet up with other ducks on the nearby lake, including Petals and others. Now fully mature, all of them would be looking for a mate as they again migrated down to the Maryland shore and Chesapeake Bay. With winter starting to prod them with more ice each day, Blossom and the nearby mallards once again started drifting literally toward the coast and on to more temperate destinations.

The prior year, she had traveled with only six young ducks. This had been a better season, having hatched thirteen eggs and watching eight mature into adults. She regretted the loss of so many of her young ones but that was the way of life, and she had beat the odds. She hoped and expected that there would be more in the future, with the help of the two leggers in paradise.

Chapter 34
Together

The winter's migration had been routine. There had been no significant events or close encounters with smoking sticks, although Blossom and Petals had heard the "booms" from areas adjacent to where they had rested and fed. Blossom had arrived at the beaver pond to find Petals there, and mother and daughter had immediately begun to catch-up on what had happened to them over the past three months. Both had found good mates, who were still accompanying them both.

Petals, remembering how Blossom had shown up at the pond the prior year with ten ducklings, asked her mom how she had been able to protect her eggs so that she had so many ducklings survive. Blossom shared that it was because of her nesting paradise at Marble Brook. Petals did not really understand what her mom was explaining, so Blossom suggested that they pay a visit to Marble Brook that evening so Petals could see what she was talking about.

With a quack to follow her, Blossom led the way, and the four headed toward Marble Brook. Circling over the ball fields and then the school building, they saw that the parking lot was empty except for two cars. The roof was almost free of any water, as it had been a dry spring so far, but Blossom still planned to land there so that they could peek into the courtyard for any other occupants.

They flew around the school twice, with Blossom and her mate leading the way and landing on the roof. Petals and her mate made another spin above the school before setting their wings and dropping down to join Blossom and her mate, who were already moving toward the roof edge next to the courtyard. As the other couple caught up with Blossom at the roof's edge, Blossom, having already surveyed the area, launched over the edge, and landed in an open grass area with her mate close behind. Petals, having seen her mom go down, did not join her immediately but took time to look over the courtyard to understand its layout and just in case Blossom might have missed something. Satisfied with what she saw, Petals and her mate joined the other pair on the ground.

Having now seen the surroundings, Petals understood what her mother had loved about Marble Brook. Cautious at first, they finally relaxed and began to explore the courtyard together. Blossom led them toward the small apple tree and the bird feeders where, instead of a water pan, there was now a small blue plastic pool. *Nice,* Blossom thought, *an upgrade.* The four of them enjoyed some of the scattered bird feed, then made a quick tour of the remaining courtyard. They decided to spend the night there so that Petals and her mate could experience the paradise more fully; so they found a resting spot for the night at the far end of the courtyard. As luck would have it, the two legger appeared in the building with its long-necked noise maker, going room to room, but outside they all rested without incident, in their peaceful spa.

Chapter 35
The Watch

Helen loved seeing nature's rebirth. Fruit began to grow on the apple tree, delicate petals started to drop, and the days were longer, so she no longer arrived and departed from school in the dark. This Friday, they had their class field trip to visit the town's historical sites on Main Street: the town library; the old meeting house, whose weathervane had musket ball marks on it from George Washington's troops using it for target practice; and, this year, they had added the community newspaper office to their tour.

She had come in early again to run off copies of the field trip permission sheets she would send home with the students today as well as to update the weekly job assignments. Ever since last spring, she could not help but peer out occasionally to see if there were any ducks in the courtyard, but so far, she had seen none. She wondered if they had traumatized the mallard hen last year, and hope was fading that she and her ducklings would return, as Helen knew that they had appeared before the Memorial Day holiday, which was next week.

As she reflected, she peered out the window again and to her delight, she saw Blossom looking up at her with another thirteen ducklings. Helen realized her appearance must have come as a surprise, and she saw the hen immediately lead her family quickly across the courtyard to the shrubs at the other end of the yard. She smiled.

Helen was thrilled to see that the ducks were back, and that the earlier incident had not scared them away. She headed to the office to let the chief and Peggy know the ducks had returned. As she entered the hallway, she saw the head custodian leaving the office, and she said, "Devin, just a minute." He turned in the direction of the voice, then responded, "Good morning, Helen. How can I help you?"

"I just wanted to give you a heads up that our mother duck is back and has a new family of ducklings," Helen shared. "Wonderful," Devin said, smiling and shaking his head. "Thanks for letting me know."

Helen left a note in the office for Betty and Principal Booker. She suspected they would want to keep the news a secret as long as possible.

Chapter 36
Surprise

Blossom was surprised to see the golden feathered two legger at the window. She had instinctively hurried away with her ducklings to find concealment under the shrubs. As she collected the ducklings under the green canopy, Blossom reminded herself that the two leggers had been helpful, and she needed to trust them. She remained cautious, though, as she still needed to keep her family out of sight of Nails and her progeny.

She soon noticed that piles of seed were again being left on the ground under the apple tree, which made feeding her ducklings easier, faster and it reduced their exposure to unwanted eyes. Other than the bird feeder crew, two leggers had not come into the courtyard since they had been seen by the golden feathered two legger at the window by the feeders. Blossom's early and late routine also kept them from being detected by Nails, who had periodically flown over the courtyard but had not yet stopped in one of the trees. As her ducklings grew and became more adventurous, Blossom knew it was only a matter of time before she and her ducklings were discovered.

Petals had decided to also nest in the courtyard, although not immediately, so she was a full two weeks behind on incubating her thirteen eggs. Her nest was located farther into the shrubs and much closer to the corner of the courtyard than her mother's. Both nests were well out of sight of the two leggers. She closely observed Blossom's routine with feeding times and keeping her brood close to the shrubs and out of sight during the daylight hours. She trusted her mom and would continue to observe her in the coming days as she waited on her own eggs to hatch. Petals was excited to know that all thirteen eggs she laid would hatch, and she would have twice as many ducklings this year as she did before.

No surprise, it was a katydid that blew the cover off the duckling secret. The insect was a fat healthy specimen who, as luck would have it, had dropped down on a low shrub branch in front of the ducklings. They reacted immediately to it, so the bug made a quick move to avoid capture by leaping with a short flight to the lawn, followed by short hopping flights across the grass tops. Three ducklings gave chase before Blossom could stop them. They were already twenty feet away from the shrubs, all stabbing at the escaping insect with their beaks with little success but causing the bug to scramble for its life.

The sudden movement in the courtyard was unfortunately seen by a little two legger, who was sharpening her pencil by the window ledge. "Hey, ducklings!" she yelled, some more two leggers joining her at the window while her teacher grimaced, knowing that getting her class back on task this afternoon was going to be an uphill battle. Fortunately, this was an early dismissal day for the Memorial Day holiday, so for now, the impact would be minimal. Still, Peggy and the chief would be giving the custodians orders to have the family removed, which they hoped would go more smoothly having now learned to concentrate on the ducklings.

During early dismissal it was evident that the duckling news was traveling fast, as the level of chatter and the number of duck announcements between students was high. The holiday break was coming at a good time so that the immediate excitement of the new ducklings would die down by the following Tuesday when students would return. Once all the buses had left, Helen took the seed bucket out to the courtyard and left some extra-large piles for the ducklings to eat over the long weekend which would spare her husband any late-night visit to restock.

That night the two legger with the long-necked noise maker made its rounds as usual, and there was a light rain that made for damp raw-feeling coolness. Blossom and her family were snuggled together tightly, peacefully enjoying their shared warmth and closeness.

Despite the conditions, there was still movement in the courtyard. Petals felt the eggs under her start to come to life with little taps, then little punctures disturbed the smooth egg surfaces. Little bodies could be felt struggling against their enclosures as she repositioned herself to help them to escape. She gently removed the broken eggshells as each new duckling made its debut. This continued all night and the following day. Petals was thrilled to feel and see her wonderful clutch hatch into thirteen beautiful fluffs of duckling. *Momma was so wise to have found such a wonderful place to nest,* Petals thought. The evidence was now snuggling up underneath her to stay warm.

On the second day Petals led her new family to the apple tree and the bird seed, where she found Blossom and her family already there. Her mother's ducklings were three times the size of Petals' newly hatched tribe. The older ducklings were not in the mood to share with their little cousins, and they chased off the smaller hatchlings. Blossom could see the concern in Petals' expression and knew that this situation could not last long, as it was critical for the younger ducks to eat soon. Fortunately, the school was quiet and peaceful the next couple of days with no rumblers or two leggers arriving. The two hens agreed to eat, feed, and water their young at different times, with Petals going first, followed by Blossom when Petals gave a call that they were finished and had moved away.

Four days later, the rumblers returned. The windows opened

soon after, and they heard the noises of the two leggers inside. Blossom knew that if fourteen ducklings had been too many at the pond, twenty-six ducklings in the courtyard was equally unsustainable, and it would surely draw the attention of the hawks again. She needed to leave so Petal's ducklings had a chance to survive and to do that, she needed help from the two leggers. *How can I do this?* she pondered.

She knew that the two legger with the golden head feathers seemed to connect with her in some unspoken way, and things had improved before from their silent exchange. When she finished eating that morning, she and her ducklings remained near the holly bush and shrubs next to the apple tree feeders. When she heard the two legger with golden feathers near the window, she moved away from the shrubs so she could be seen and heard, giving soft quacks of greeting. At first nothing happened, but then it appeared and looked directly at her with a bright expression. Blossom tilted her head so that her right eye was looking directly into the eyes of the two legger in the window, and they held each other's attention for a moment. They seemed to look at each other not with fear, but with understanding. It was time to move on.

Chapter 37
Help

Custodian Devin had just returned to his office from having talked to the chief, who had told him that Principal Booker wanted him to remove the ducklings as soon as possible, and his phone was ringing. He picked it up and recognized Helen's voice on the other end. "Devin, I wanted to let you know that the mother duck is acting like she wants to leave the courtyard. She was just under my window, quacking, and then she took her ducklings and headed to the landing step in front of the door that leads out of the courtyard. Do you think we could let them out?" Devin did not hesitate; this was too good to be true. "Yes, I will head there now." "Thanks, Devin," Helen said, and they both hung up.

The mother duck and her thirteen ducklings were huddled up near the courtyard doors when Devin got to the entrance hallway. He pulled both center corridor doors closed to isolate the entrance hall, set the outside entrance door in the open position, and then he walked to the interior courtyard door and pushed it open. Devin intended to leave it open by locking the door closer in the open position as he had done on the exterior, and then he would retreat back into one of the corridor doors to let them pass. The duck family did not want to wait for that. Immediately they were jumping up and over the open door's threshold and proceeding to the other end and out onto the playground. There was a class enjoying recess outside and he signaled the teacher on duty, Mrs. Pogue, to help him clear the path to the fields so that the mallard mother and her ducklings could escape unimpeded. The students gathered round to see the little parade, cheering as a trio of straggling ducklings kept sprinting forward, trying to keep up with the larger group.

Word of the exit of the mallard family quickly traveled the schoolwide grapevine, as so many had witnessed them parade across the playing fields to the duck pond. The secret of their presence had been kept so successfully that many students would have suggested that it was just a rumor, however, there were too many personal testimonies as to the event that it was beyond question that Marble Brook had indeed been home to thirteen ducklings a second time.

Chapter 38
Making Room

Blossom's heart was pounding, as her plan had worked out better than she had hoped, and the two leggers again had helped her and her ducklings. She did not understand the sounds they made, but they appeared to understand her. It was amazing. Simply amazing. Now Petals and her ducklings would have the food they needed and have less of a chance of being discovered by the hawks. She realized there were still going to be a lot of challenges at the pond and their survival strategies would have to be different, but there would be more high protein bugs and foods for her own ducklings outside the courtyard, so she knew she had done the right thing for them all.

Petals had watched this all transpire in a matter of minutes. She heard her mother talking to the two legger with the golden feathers at the window about her needing to leave the courtyard so that Petals and her ducklings could have enough space and opportunity to eat and grow before they faced the outside world.

She watched Blossom escort her ducklings to the concrete ledge in front of the glass door, and then when the opening appeared, her mother had not hesitated to lead her troop through it and into the building. She hoped that Blossom and her ducklings were still safe but, in her heart, she knew that her mom had a good reason for leaving.

What courage Blossom demonstrated. She had to expose herself to the two leggers that way for Petals and her ducklings' benefit. Her mom was amazing, and Petals felt overwhelmed by the knowledge that she and her ducklings were all loved. Alone for the first time with her ducklings in the courtyard, it was up to her to figure things out. She hoped she too would have the courage like her mom when the time would come to leave.

Devin was glad to see the hen and her ducklings hit the path that led to the beaver pond. Thanks to Helen, he was able to seize the opportunity to extricate the ducks in less than thirty minutes. Principal Booker and the chief had a new appreciation for his ability to get things done quickly. Now the school could focus on the year end tasks at hand without the distraction of the ducks.

Now that the ducklings were no longer there, Helen did not put out additional seed for the weekend.

Chapter 39
Alone

P etals missed having her mom nearby as night enveloped the courtyard. Despite having thirteen little ones holding close to her, she felt a sort of loneliness and melancholy. The two legger's nightly noise routine came and went, and she and her ducklings settled into the routine pattern that Blossom had followed.

She was surprised after the yellow rumblers had left one day, when the courtyard doors opened and a large two legger entered the yard with a large noise maker that started chewing the grass off evenly across the yard. Her ducklings started peeping with fear as the two legger and the noise maker moved across the courtyard, starting on the end near the bird feeders, then slowly moving back and forth across the courtyard and under the shrubs on each side.

The sound and the duckling anxiety, along with Petals' concern, grew as the noise maker kept getting closer and closer to their end of the yard. Petals moved them to her nest area in the far corner as the two legger approached, and when it went to the opposite side of the yard, she and the ducklings made a break for the other end, hiding underneath the shrubs on the opposite side.

The two legger was looking away from them, toward where the noise maker was moving, so their exodus went undetected, and their peeps and her quacks were drowned out. The racket suddenly stopped and the two legger pushed the now silent noise maker to the doorway and back into the building, leaving the grass an even height and the courtyard quiet again. *Well, that was a surprise. I wonder if there will be any more coming.*

The next morning Petals noticed that there was far less bird seed under the apple tree than she had grown accustomed to seeing. The next few days, the school was quiet, inside, and out. No rumblers or two leggers were heard, which had happened on a regular basis before, so Petals was not concerned. But they were having to search harder to find enough food to satisfy the ducklings appetites which was worrisome.

Then the rumblers appeared, and the windows opened, and there were the sights and sounds of two leggers inside and outside, with one or two large two leggers coming to the concrete bench and patio area in the courtyard. With this development, Petals kept her and the ducklings in the corner away from any wandering two-legger eyes. Her ducklings, however, sensed her concern and peeped their own fear at the presence of two leggers in such great numbers in their courtyard home.

Petals saw the bird feeder crew come and go, so the availability of seed on the ground improved during the week, but it was still far less than they had enjoyed before Blossom had escaped with her brood. *What has changed?* she wondered. Then again for two days, the rumblers did not come, and the school was quiet. This time, the ducklings stayed hungry and scratched around to find anything to eat. *What would Momma do?* Petals knew that Blossom had talked to the two legger with the golden head feathers when she needed help. Could she do that? Blossom knew how to talk to the two legger and make it understand. *What if I say the wrong thing?* she fretted, her thoughts interrupted by the hungry peeps of her ducklings. She had no choice. She had to try for her ducklings.

The following morning, she and the ducklings stayed close to the holly bush and shrubs beside the feeders. When the windows opened out and she heard the little two leggers inside, she moved into the yard so she was more visible to the creatures inside the school. A small two legger happened to be by the window ledge, and she looked at Petals and her ducklings.

Petals saw a couple of small two leggers go to the feeders and fill them later that morning, and she also noticed that they had poured several piles of seed on the ground under the apple tree. The two legger with the golden feathers had looked at her when she was talking, and as with her mother, she appeared to have understood that she was pleading for food for her babies. *These two leggers have been kind and helpful, but why? How and why did they learn our duck language? Did Momma teach it to them?* Although she had many questions, she was also very thankful that the golden feathered two legger had understood and now more food was being left for them.

Chapter 40
New News

Little Connie was returning a book to the container by the window ledge, when she spotted a large duck and her ducklings waddling in the courtyard. Seeing Helen through the classroom window, she called out, "Mrs. Dean, I see the mother duck is back with her ducklings." "That's impossible!" Helen said. "See! They are right there," the girl persisted.

Helen joined Connie at the window and saw that indeed there was a mallard hen, cocking her head and looking directly at her, quacking softly, with thirteen ducklings scurrying around her. How was this possible? The chief had told her that Devin had moved the mother and ducklings to the pond. Had the chief said that as a ruse to divert attention from the ducklings? Surely not. *Why would they lie to us?* Helen thought. *This must be another mother duck.*

Helen remembered that the first hen had a patch that was a beautiful dark shade of sapphire, but this hen's wing patch had a tint of amethyst purple. She was surprised, realizing that they had had two mallards hatch eggs in the courtyard. Twenty-six ducklings in the space of a week. With class starting in only two minutes, she quickly picked up her classroom phone and called the office to give them the news. For now, extra seed piles would be added to the bird feeder team's instructions.

Chapter 41
Keep Moving

Blossom and her ducklings found the beaver pond area the same as she had left it the prior year. Fortunately, the geese and gadwalls had not chosen to nest there again. This was good news, as it meant that for now, she and her brood would have adequate food and cover to support them all.

This was only good for the short term, as in a week or two, Blossom fully expected there would be twice the ducks needing to be fed and that number would not be sustainable there.

Considering all the alternatives and the capabilities of her family, Blossom decided the best course of action was for them to go to the river that she had often visited, and where she had taken her older ducklings late the prior year when they could fly. Now they would have to walk or swim to a new home.

She decided they would stay at the pond for now, but when conditions were right, they would set out to find their way along the small stream that flowed out of the beaver pond down to the river. This could be a treacherous journey, but she needed to make the move so that Petal's ducklings had a better chance of surviving on what the pond ecosystem could provide. Besides, the journey to the river would be easier for her more developed ducklings than Petal's young.

Blossom recognized or saw signs of all the long-time residents of the beaver pond. Chomps and Cuddles were not in view, but she was sure they were lurking below the surface while frogs and tadpoles moved around in the shallows. Beak, using typical heron tactics, stood like a statue, awaiting the appearance of an amphibian that it could spear with a single thrust.

Blossom's family took to the pond naturally, enjoying the much larger water area than the pool they left behind in the courtyard. Fair mild days ensued as the plant and tree growth continued to thicken.

After a long dry spell at the pond, a warm steady rain began to fall in the late afternoon and continued overnight and into the next day. Caused by a slow retreating warm front, the wet weather started without any wind. As the soft rain fell, the pond water level began to rise and spill over the beaver dams, forming into gentle but sustained flow down a small stream wetland depression. Blossom felt she should be seeing Petals soon. The rain collected in large drops on her back, and then slid down her wings so she decided that conditions were now ideal for them to move to the river by floating around the perimeter of the ball fields on the beaver pond's outflow as trekked slowly downhill toward the river.

The stream eventually met a residential road, where it flowed along in a ditch in front of neatly kept houses and lawns, with driveways crossing the ditch at intervals. Had they been traveling during dry weather conditions, this part of the journey would have presented a greater challenge, as two houses had dogs and one a cat. Fortunately, these four-legged problems were dry and warm behind closed doors and not pursuing what to them would have appeared to be trespassers in their individual domains. The duck column simply floated down the ditch through the driveway, crossing culverts until they came to a grate that let the water cascade down through it into a deep pit located at the corner, where the road met a much larger roadway. On the large roadway, there was an intermittent flow of rumblers of all types and sizes passing by in both directions, throwing spray behind them as they went. Where the stream went to in the pit was a mystery, and the grate openings were too small for Blossom. At that point, she steered her entourage away from it and any unseen dangers, heading to the edge of the roadway where they were totally exposed.

Thankfully, with the steady rain, no hawks were roaming the sky above, so she felt safe enough in that risk category. The rumblers presented a different and immediate danger, though. They were expressionless and seemed unstoppable, except at regular intervals when they would stop on their own volition in a single line. Then, like a column of ducklings, they would all start moving at the same time. They all had big smooth eyes with long tail-like appendages whipping back and forth over them. Oddly, no matter the size, color, and shape, all the rumblers seemed to have that one trait in common.

Her ducklings were becoming anxious the longer they stayed next to the roadway near the rumblers, so Blossom moved them up a grassy slope and next to a low wall to allow her time to figure out how to proceed to the river. After a few minutes, she concluded that periodically the rumblers would all stop for a specific amount of time. She thought that it would be long enough for them to cross, her reasoning being that stopped rumblers were easier to avoid than moving rumblers.

Finally, deciding that it was now or never, Blossom swiftly moved them all back down the grass slope to the roadway as the group of rumblers came to a stop, and they briskly scrambled across. When they had made it halfway, a rumbler appeared from the other direction, sending a fright through the group as it slid to a stop only inches from the trailing ducklings. Everyone went into a frantic sprint across the roadway in front, under and behind one of the stopped rumblers. They gathered with stressed peeps around Blossom on the sidewalk on the opposite side of the road, which ran along another walled embankment. Blossom moved downhill on the sidewalk as the panic-stricken ducklings fought to stay as close to her as possible. At the lower end of the sidewalk, they came to another road which was fortunately clear of rumblers. Blossom hopped off the curb and down onto the street, and the ducklings followed her without hesitation. The tight cluster of ducks quickly waddled their way across the wet pavement into an area full of quiet resting rumblers.

Weaving their way around the idle rumblers and down the sloping paved area, they came to a small grass plot next to the river. On it were some large white trunks, sitting on a smooth flat ledge area, with a surface like the patio in the courtyard at Marble Brook. She could hear the rapids of the stream behind the white trunks. The group circled the flat ledge and came to a wood fence with steel wire strung between and attached to its posts. The wire mesh was too small for Blossom and the ducklings to go through it, so they continued to follow the fence downstream to its end, where the parking lot run-off now flowed down a small washed-out gully that dropped to the river's edge. Blossom flapped her wings and settled on the river's edge while the ducklings followed, some sliding down on their tails, others tumbling down the slope to the water. They had made it, and Blossom was thankful she had not lost any of her babies along the way.

Chapter 42
The Tree

The large hemlock had succumbed to an invasive insect from Honshu, Japan, called the wooly adelgid. The invader had journeyed inside a pallet used to import manufactured goods from Asia; goods that once had been made in water powered plants that sat along small New England streams during the Industrial Revolution. Now those old red brick New England plant structures were slowly decaying and collapsing, as roofs failed, and owners neglected upkeep. A lack of tenants was common due to the limited amenities and parking these sites had since they were often located in ravines where dams could be easily built, and the nearby stream's waterpower was harnessed.

The beetle infestation had killed whole stands of these native conifers. Despite its size, the beetles had weakened the tree. Slowly, its branches lost life and their foliage, the fine soft sprays of needles died and dropped; woodpeckers started boring into the bark, making larger holes for nests, all the while the sound of winds blowing through its green fingers was systematically silenced. The limbs began to rot and break off from their own weight, leaving a naked spiked trunk with bark still clinging in mottled patches.

A wood duck had taken over a pileated woodpecker's hole on the underside of the lower trunk, which was much larger and more accommodating than its smaller wood hammering cousins' domiciles that were hollowed out in other parts of the dead tree. The location of the duck's nest leaning over the stream flow had been perfect for her and her mate to safely raise three groups of ducklings. When the young ducks fledged and left the nest, they easily survived the fifteen-foot drop to a splashy landing in the stream's eddy pool below.

It was a winter Northeaster that had finally toppled the giant, with its tilt toward and over the stream, where in healthier times it could capture more sun in the air space created by the water. The weight of ice and snow coupled with the forty mile an hour wind gusts rocking it back and forth, along with the dead roots which had been undercut by the river finally broke loose, releasing their tenacious hold on the rocky ledge. The towering sentinel finally had yielded to gravity and wind.

Without the wind shield of other healthy trees, the icy weight and a hard gust of wind drove its top upstream toward the opposite riverbank. As the treetop's weight leveraged the force on the roots, it pulled the base out enough for it to slide off and down the six-foot rock ledge into the stream. This impact that sent a powerful energy wave through the tree's spine, whipping off most of the remaining dead limbs. Continuing to fall toward the opposite hillside's ledge, the massive tree thrashed and splayed smaller trees as it fell. The tree's angular velocity coupled with the mass of the lower trunk, snapped the twenty-four-inch mid-section cleanly apart and it flipped a twenty foot one-thousand-pound section of the upper trunk through the air. The trunk landing on the larger end, balanced momentarily upright as if it wanted to hold its head high one last time, and then it dropped onto the shelf ice along the stream's edge with a final gravel crunching crash, smashing the shelf ice, shooting fragments skittering across the frozen terrain.

Beyond the Pond

The behemoth was at rest with the stream's quiet soft gurgle, welcoming its fallen neighbor who now rested on its stream bed. Fortunately, the end occurred at a time when it did not have any nesting residents occupying its trunk, and the few wintering occupants had all been able to escape.

Chapter 43
The Flood

Thunderstorms trained in a line along a slow-moving spring cold front that had crawled to a stop along the New England coast. The system had dropped over seven inches of rain in only twenty-four hours. Although historically a farming community, the area in the past forty years had changed, with government officials interested in increasing the tax base through economic development and new homes. Construction designs favored shedding any precipitation liquid or snow melt as fast as possible from yards into the streets and storm drains. New residential streets, high density housing, and shopping centers, with all their roofs, sidewalks, parking lots, and connecting roadways now took rainfall from 14 percent of the land area on an express route to the river. This unimpeded flow turned the river from a gentle flowing brook to a raging torrent in a matter of minutes during a normal thunderstorm. It was like going from a water hose to a firehose to water your flower beds, and the result would not be pretty. This storm had amplified that effect, as the land had all the water it could absorb under the deluge that continued to fall.

The rising water awoke the behemoth from its watery bed; its root wad now resting downstream, sitting over a scoured-out depression caused by turbulence from the river flow being accelerated around its fan of decaying roots. When the stormwater express roared through the narrow ravine, the equivalent of five fully loaded Class A tanker trucks of water started passing by every second. The upstream section of the trunk not yet waterlogged had enough buoyancy to be lifted off the bottom by the rising flow. The log's inertia resisted the water express's force, at first creating a frothing turbulence on its upstream side. Slowly, the forty-four-foot trunk section began moving and gained speed in the rising water's flow. In short order, the tree trunk was moving at the velocity of the stream, whose surging waters angrily chewed at and overran the riverbanks. The stream was no longer a peaceful gurgle but a deep violent torrent of rapids blasting through and around anything opposing its downhill charge and underappreciated power.

Blossom had moved her brood to the island above the dam the prior night since it provided a safe and isolated area to roost. The most violent weather had started at first light. The daylight was later than normal due to the heavy weather's low cloud cover. Once it started, the heavy rain was intense and constant, not like a typical downpour that lasted only four or five minutes. The water level rose quickly, covering the island within a matter of minutes. As it deepened, the highest velocity water was starting to take the shortest route to the dam, which was over top of the island. With the water and debris now charging at them, the island was not going to be safe for long. Blossom decided to move them to the quieter eddy on the opposite side of the river just above the dam where water remained flat and slower. While they still could, she needed to lead her family upstream so that they had enough distance and the necessary angle for paddling safely across the strong current and avoid being pulled over the dam. She had been concentrating on keeping her brood in a tight grouping as they crossed over the flat deep heavy current, moving through the pool above the dam, when too late she realized it was there.

The roots of a very large log rose out of the upwelling current in front of them, cutting them off from the eddy. The log's large root mass then hit the concrete dam's spillway wall, causing the rest of the log to be forced up to the surface as the racing torrent rose to crest the dam. This also resulted in the upper trunk rotating toward them, pushing a churn of wood, debris, and trash ahead of it. Blossom and the ducklings paddled hard, but the log's trunk now pivoting and sweeping across the channel drove them back into the fastest current and toward the dam's spillway. She had no choice but to go airborne and watch her thirteen ducklings be swept over the edge of the four-story high dam.

The puffs of brown and yellow disappeared over the roaring spillway, their momentum tossing them into the misty chaos of falling water and debris. The dam's face was steeply angled, resulting in a literal free fall of forty feet into the foaming boil of its rocky splash pool below. Close behind, the log followed, sure to smash some, if not all, the ducklings to oblivion.

Chapter 44
Wondering

Helen and her husband had planned to take their boat out on the lake for the first time this year, but that was not to be. Conditions on the lake, with the continued heavy rain that had just hit, were sure to have created an ugly brown water mixture of trash and limbs, interspersed with water-soaked logs, and the rising lake level would have lifted off the banks and been pushed out of inlets by swollen streams and dumped into the water.

Always the master of the obvious, Helen's husband stated, "Today is duck weather. Best we stay warm and dry at home." "Good call, Honey" she responded, having decided that already the prior night when she had seen the forecast on his favorite entertainment, the Weather Channel.

Still, his comment about duck weather made her wonder how the two momma ducks and their ducklings were doing.

Chapter 45
The Ride

As the upper portion of the log dropped over the edge, the large roots were caught by the lip of the spillway. Instead of tumbling straight over and down the falls, they now hooked on to the top corner of the dam, forcing the rest of the log to swing across the dam face like a pendulum, crashing into the downstream armored wall and coming to rest, leaning against the dam upside down with the root wad at the top corner of the spillway. The roots blocked the water as it overtopped the dam, creating an umbrella of spray and froth that contrasted to the smooth curtain of water cascading down the rest of the spillway.

"Wow, what a ride," peeped one duckling. They had not noticed the log's crash over the dam in the mist and spray atmosphere of the thundering torrent below the dam.

"Let's do it again," said one of the other ducklings, shaking off the beads of spray from his head and beak. "Where's Mom? I hope she is alright."

Blossom had had no choice but to fly so as not to be hurdled over the spillway to her death. Landing downstream of the dam, she looked back to see if she could spot any of her babies. As she called for them, she saw three survivors float past her, then four more. She called again, and they eagerly paddled across the current to her. Another group of five appeared and joined the group. One was still missing. She led the group she had gathered to a patch of slack water, then flew back upstream to the dam plunge pool. She did not see the missing one. The cloud of spray and foam from the unstoppable flow reduced visibility to only an intermittent glimpse of two or three feet at best, so her duckling could have easily been caught in an undertow and pinned against the large rocks in the plunge pool. She flew up and over the cloud of spray to the bluff side of the spillway. Then she saw him. He was almost under the falls deluge, trying to get up out of the water onto the concrete ledge step at the dam's spillway base. Blossom called him, but he seemed to be ignoring her, so she half flew and paddled up to him and gave him a gentle peck, grateful he was unhurt and alive.

"Hey, Mom. I want to do it again. Can I?" "Sorry, but this ride is over, and we need to join the others," Blossom responded.

"Why can't I do it again?" he protested.

Because ducklings don't fly, she thought. Ignoring his question, she nudged him away from the spillway, and they both rode the rolling current downstream to join the other ducklings.

Blossom knew that the river led to a large lake and that the ravine, with its falling terrain along the way, did not provide suitable habitat for raising her family. Since the ducklings would not be flying soon, the only practical option was to ride the flood down to the lake and face the swans. The much larger waterfowl were beautiful birds, but they bullied their smaller duck cousins.

They moved swiftly with the flood downstream, and the water made a quick right as it now exploded off a twelve-foot-high ledge of rock. The ducklings did not hesitate as they headed to the drop off. Unlike the dam's smooth even face, this ledge consisted of an irregular outcropping of rock that resulted in less of a free fall;

consisted mostly of a series of splashy bounces and tumbles before finding a deeper pool at its base. The ducklings loved it, and Blossom flew over the falls and joined her happy flotilla, riding high on the torrent until the flood waters had spent their energy and slipped into the calm, back water of the lake, still moving but on a flat, powerful, much quieter flow.

Chapter 46
Ducklings

They watched as the hen and her ducklings came up the lawn from the lake. They had seen goslings and cygnets in the yard before, but not ducklings. Michael remembered the ducklings at school when he was in Mrs. Dean's class. They would feed the birds, and, last spring, a mother duck had nested in the courtyard. Ironically, he was seeing the same duck now, but he did not realize it.

He should find their cat to ensure he did not attack the new visitors to their yard. Fortunately, Oreo was curled up on top of the ottoman in the family room. Michael could tell that the mother duck was frantically looking over her shoulder at the neighbor's little shih tzu, who barked incessantly behind his electronic fence at anything that moved.

"Mom, come look, ducklings," Michael yelled.

Michael's mom joined her son, and she smiled as she saw the orange beak of the mallard, her baker's dozen pecking their way through the yard. "Mom, do we have any bread I can feed them?" "I do, but we should not feed them bread, as it is unhealthy for them, I am told, for the ducklings especially."

Bald eagles roosted nearby, cruising the sky overhead. Hawks were one thing; an eagle was a threat to both Blossom and the ducklings. Hopefully, the eagles were finding plenty of food below the power dam located a mile up the lake. There, fish in the lake above the dam would be sucked through the power turbine and float up to the surface, stunned and easy pickings for the eagles. So hopefully they did not need to supplement their diet with other types of meat. It was amazing, Blossom reflected, that despite all the recent events, her thirteen ducklings had survived, and now they found themselves on something so much bigger than the beaver pond.

That afternoon, while shopping for the week's groceries, Michael pleaded, "Mom, can we buy some birdseed like we bought for Mrs. Dean's class?" "Sure, Honey, let's see what they have."

Chapter 47
The Survivors

Things had gone well for Petals and her ducklings since she had talked to the two legger. Food was plentiful and except for the bird feeder crew, the two leggers seldom entered the courtyard. During the heavy rain storm the kiddie pool was filled to its brim and as the ducklings swam in it, their little waves caused water to slosh over its sides.

The intense rainfall had converted the courtyard into a shallow pond, as the ground drains became partially clogged with leaves and mulch that had been floated by the gathering water. Although a problem for many other creatures, Petals and her ducklings were well equipped to survive this event. Much of the birdseed was floating around the yard so the ducklings simply swam around to find it. Within two hours of the rain stopping, the courtyard grass reappeared, and things returned to a soggy normal.

With plenty of food, her thirteen ducklings grew quickly. As feared, a young male hawk, smaller than Nails, who had targeted Blossom's first Marble Brook brood, landed on a lower branch of the courtyard tree. Petals did not see him at first but when he let out that characteristic screech, she moved away from the edge of the shrubs to pull her babies to a more concealed position.

As had happened to Blossom and her ducklings with Nails, the young hawk's screech terrified her ducklings and one of them bolted, their fear giving uncontrollable commands to its legs to run. The hawk was pleased, as its threatening call had had the desired effect. It gauged the ducklings' speed and direction, launching itself off the limb and setting its wings for a controlled glide, quickly gaining on its slower moving short-legged prey.

Suddenly, the hawk saw a large object hitting it on its right shoulder, knocking him sideways and over with his back toward the ground. "Quack, quack, quaaaaa-ck, quack," Petals blurted at the intruder, her larger and heavier body driving violently into the assassin.

The hawk was confused at first, going from being the attacker to now being attacked. His parents had never talked to him about mad mother ducks. This was going very badly and if he did not do something fast, he was going to the mat for the final count. He finally reacted by clasping his talons on Petal's left wing and planting the other into her breast, digging the pin sharp points into feathers and flesh. She felt stabs of pain, but she welcomed him to hold on so that she would drive him hard into the ground and to his next life.

As the mother duck blurted at him and drove him down, flapping her wings and using her weight to drop them both to the ground, the hawk released his grip on Petals and, as best he could, pushed off her, falling backwards into a tall bush. He immediately regrouped himself and attempted to fly upward to escape the unexpected terror.

When Petal's feet hit the ground, she relaunched herself and targeted him again in the bush. Winded by the first impact, he fought to unfold his wings, but Petals planted her orange beak squarely on his breast plate, causing him to start spastic flapping of his wings to escape, which he did as the heavier hen fell into the bush, and then dropped to the ground.

All the while, the ducklings were peeping and huddling in panic, with the errant duckling joining them as they watched the spectacle of Petals and the hawk in combat. Mom was mad. Every duckling now knew they needed to do what she said, or the consequences could be painful for sure. Where and when were they going to learn her version of duck jujitsu?

It took a moment for Petals to collect herself. Her body literally shuddered with energy as her fight reflex subsided. What had overcome her? Never had she felt such aggression towards anything. Her heart was pounding so hard she felt as if her head might explode, but she finally breathed in deeply and started to relax. Regaining awareness of her surroundings, she realized that her youngsters were once again snuggling up next to her. She nervously quacked to calm her own state of excitement, but the ducklings could feel the emotional tension still coursing through every part of her being.

Petals moved them deeper into the shrub cover in case the hawk or one of its friends came back. She did not realize that the hawk was not planning on ever returning to the courtyard.

That evening as they went to the feeders, Petals felt the wounds she had received in the fight with the young hawk. The stiffness in her breast and forewing were the most uncomfortable. It was worth it, though, to still have all thirteen of her little ones alive and around her now, eating and diving in the kiddie pool. Blossom would be proud to know that her sweet Petals had inherited her mother's courage and that raptor school would be adding a new topic to their curriculum: Why you should avoid mad mother ducks.

Petals reflected on the hawk encounter and although there had not been any new appearances, she realized, as her mother did before her, that time was running out for her and the ducklings to remain in the courtyard. Thanks to her mom, Petals knew what she needed to do now.

Chapter 48
Year Done

School was out for the summer, and Helen was still in her room stowing her materials and clearing all the surfaces and floor so that the custodians could come in to do a deep cleaning and make any needed repairs and touch-ups to paint and varnish.

As she methodically processed the room, she reflected on the past year. She had had what must have been the best class ever, despite many having allergies. The class average score on the standardized tests, along with the other second grade classes, was well above the district and state average, and they all had worked hard on their studies.

The parents had also been so supportive and proactively offered help, and her parent volunteers had blown her away with their creativity and generosity with an amazing gift certificate to one of her favorite dress shops. There had also been many individual gifts with sweet notes. Her favorite was a message from Tim, who wrote, "Thank you, Mrs. Dean, you are the Beast Teacher ever." She smiled.

They created great memories and had made her job fun in a

very special way. The only real negative was her finding out how she had failed to understand what had happened between Randy Jackson and Danielle Young the prior year with the hornet. She had to let that go, but it still left a mark on her heart that she had failed them. Thankfully, she took comfort in Peggy's kind words of challenge and encouragement to use the experience to recognize that no one can be perfect.

Thinking about feeding the birds reminded her that this year they had twenty-six ducklings hatch in the courtyard. *Amazing!* Helen smiled as she remembered both mother ducks outside her window, with all their little fuzzy babies scurrying about them. It was a marvel to see animals adapt to different surroundings and still thrive. One could not help but wonder, hope, that both hens would be back next spring.

"Enough!" she finally said out loud, then gathered her purse and box of items and headed home for the summer rest and a trip to Italy to visit friends and experience the Amalfi coast.

Chapter 49
Wondering

When she arrived at the beaver pond with her thirteen ducklings, Petals was surprised and worried that her mother was nowhere to be found. She had followed her mom's example, and the two leggers had made it easy to leave the courtyard through the tunnel to the outside. She was scared that Blossom and her ducklings had not made it out alive earlier, but when it turned out to be so easy to leave with the two-leggers' help, she could not avoid looking forward to catching up with her. Petals hoped they were just hiding somewhere because there was some new predator around.

Her ducklings, however, were not burdened with any disappointment, as they loved the wider expanse of deep water the pond provided. Her little downy bubbles of life had disappeared under the surface, then popped back up, down, up, down, up, in non-stop motion, playing tag. Keeping track of them all was impossible, and Petals hoped that when their game was done, she would still be able to count thirteen babies. Seeing the new arrivals, Chomps' eyes brightened as she gave a knowing snapper smirk toward Cuddles and said, "They are back, and more than ever!"

The weeks went by, and Petal's ducklings continued to grow. Despite trying to avoid areas she was certain the snapping turtles preferred, she still found one day that her brood had been reduced to twelve. A loss for sure, but twelve was an amazing number to have, and it would not have happened were it not for the courtyard nest. Petals now resigned herself that she was not going to see her mother again. There was still a glimmer of hope, but she had to bury that emptiness caused by Blossom's disappearance. She knew she must now pay attention to her current family and take care of them and herself.

At the same time, Blossom was wondering if Petals had been able to escape the courtyard. Her intuition told her yes. She firmly believed that the two leggers understood what she had told them and would help Petals and her babies escape to the pond.

Her family did well at the lake thanks to Michael's birdseed and ensuring that no stray animals bothered her family. He put more seed out by the dock daily and that, coupled with the plentiful natural supply of grass and water plants, terrestrial and water bugs, small fish, snails, and macro invertebrates, ensured the ducklings were growing fast and big. The lake was proving to be much better than she had hoped. There still were plenty of mostly avian threats and obnoxious swan bullies, but with the dock structures and large water area, there were counter measures they could take to avoid all threats from land, sky, or water.

Chapter 50
Italy

Helen was enjoying the cool breeze in the shade and the sea view, as small crafts and water taxis ferried tourists across from the port to destinations on other parts of the Amalfi coastline. She was recovering from the scorching, hot tour of old Pompeii, Italy. The history of the ancient structures and roadways dug out of the ash from Mount Vesuvius was of great interest, but they had drawn the short straw for a guide, who weighed at least a hundred pounds more than was healthy, and she was sure that she and James had not seen all the things other tour groups were seeing because he was not physically capable of handling the radiant heat coming off all the stone and rock structures. This was compounded by there being no wind at all to help cool one's body. On their return bus ride to the Hotel Sorrento, one would have thought the guide had died from his slumped over posture in the front seat. Instead of providing local historical facts, he had snored the whole way back to the hotel.

It had been a great trip, having spent a little time near Boulogne with friends who had rented a villa, where they spent some time with their youngest son and his friends, who were making their own tour of Italy by staying at hostels. They had then taken a slow train ride over the spine of the Italian peninsula to visit the Amalfi coast. Having ridden trains in Sweden and Denmark, they were taken aback to find the train cars being rather spartan and not very substantial nor climate controlled. Despite the train's lack of comfort and amenities, they did make it to Naples and their transfer to the Hotel Sorrento.

On Helen and James first day they took a bus tour along the narrow roadway that ran along the Amalfi coast. The first part of the trip had been intense. The lane they were in ran right on the edge of a cliff. When their bus met another tour bus going the opposite direction, it felt like they might tip over the edge if the other bus clipped them. The stairways in Positano, the compact town centers, churches, shops, and eateries were all crowded with tourists. The gondola ride to the top of a hill to see the panorama of the coastline and ocean had been wonderful.

The second day, they went to the island of Capri, where they took an excursion to the blue grotto. Their guide squeezed their small dingy through a tight rock portal, and they bent down below the gunwales to avoid head injury. Waves bounced them as they passed through the little tunnel through the rock face and into a water cave, which with the light pouring in through the entrance gave a marvelous iridescent blue water effect.

Their excursion to the blue grotto had pushed the time limit for their boat back to Sorrento, and when they disembarked from the small excursion boat, they saw their primary tour vessel still at the far end of the quay. They took off in a dead run, dodging people, pets, carts, light poles, and other obstacles all the way down the dockside, with James arriving at the gangway just as they were beginning to lift it. He asked them to hold it for thirty seconds so Helen could make it and they could board together. She made it, winded, but they had both made it.

James told her that a table was waiting for them in the hotel's restaurant. Holding hands, they walked up to the restaurant entrance and a very kind maître d' seated them at a window table for two that provided an unobstructed view of the ocean.

The waiter appeared and welcomed them, then asked if they would care for any drinks. Having been dehydrated by the afternoon's boat excursion without anything to drink and then the return sprint to catch the boat, they both ordered some sparkling water with limes. The waiter shared the evening specials, which after hearing them neither of them could remember what he said, most likely because they were low on electrolytes.

Her husband smiled and looked at her and said, "Did you understand any of that?" She started to laugh, then caught herself before the whole restaurant looked their way. They ordered and enjoyed their meals, watching the harbor traffic move in and out.

Helen's phone had vibrated during dinner, but she had ignored it on principle. As they waited for their check, she decided to look at it. The message was not unexpected, but it still ruined her good mood. The town budget had finally been approved on the third vote and as a result, they were reducing the number of second grade classes at Marble Brook, and she was being moved to third grade. It was only two weeks till she had to report to work. Everything she had done to be prepared for the new school year was for naught. In the next eighteen days, she would have to learn the third-grade curriculum, move to a new classroom, and be ready to teach her new students on the first day of school. She felt panic start to set in. They would be heading home in two days, which would only leave two weeks to prep and with not much time to adjust to the jet lag from the six-hour time adjustment.

Chapter 51
Joy

Blossom felt good as she and her young took off from the lake and flew upstream and over the large dam that backed up another seven-mile-long lake. Their flock of fourteen circled around the largest part of the lake, looking for a place to safely land, and finally deciding on a cove just above the dam that had some shallows with visible underwater plants. It was time for her to let them start discovering more of the world on their own. Her plan was to start leaving them from time to time so that they became more independent and self-reliant. They all started to feed on the underwater plants and organisms. Several white tails were pointed skyward as the ducks took turns eating and watching. As they to work over the underwater grass bed, the sound of a water noise maker soon started bearing down on their location.

A group of two-leggers plowed around the lake in a vessel, creating large waves. The swells crashed into shoreline, eroding the banks and stirring up the silt in the shallow areas. The ducks did not feel much at first as the pressure of the waves approached, but as they hit the shallows area where they were feeding, the crest suddenly seemed to build to almost two feet in height. Despite their best efforts, the ducks decided that flight was better than being tumbled in the artificial surf. Loud sounds came from the two-leggers as the boat completed a hard turn and headed again back in the direction it came, pounding back through the waves it had just created coming into the cove.

Leaving the boat and lake behind, Blossom's clan cleared the dam by a hundred feet, and then started a casual glide toward their home on the river tailwater channel. The young ones could not help but crowd each other and weave back and forth in playful aerial acrobatics. Blossom realized that they were still maturing but hoped they would keep that spirit of fun and carefree adventure. She knew too well that they would have to face many things she hadn't, as the surrounding environment would continue to change and evolve. Hopefully, they would be able to adapt.

Early the next morning, Blossom swam away, and when she had put a dock between her and the young ducks, she took off flying just above the water for several hundred feet, hugging to the near shore before arching up into the summer morning's sky behind a tall tree, shielding her ascent from the young eyes of those she left behind. She was on a mission to see if her instincts were right. As she circled over the small lakeside community of homes, she headed toward the river and then Marble Brook.

As she flew, she saw that the large log was still leaning up against the narrow dam's spillway, like an umbrella left beside a front door. The river was flowing at its normal calm summer flow, and a thin curtain of water was flowing down the dam's face. Climbing in altitude as she followed the hillside to Marble Brook, she soon saw the familiar building and adjoining ball fields and play area appear.

Petals was watching her ten young ducks testing out their wings and playing tag around the pond, learning how to lift themselves up off the water. There was lots of splashing and playful quacking, which really was not the smartest thing to do early in the morning when hungry stomachs often spoke the loudest to their owners. Suddenly, Petals saw movement behind the treetops and was going to quack a warning when she recognized the familiar silhouette of another duck. It continued to track around the pond area, and then banked sharply into the light warm morning breeze and descended in a smooth gentle arc to land in the pond. Her heart pumped with pure emotion as she recognized the orange beak and loving eyes of her mom.

As she flew to join Blossom in the middle of the pond, her mother raised up, flapping her wings with joy at seeing her precious daughter. They had both survived! They began to share their experiences since the day that Blossom had left the courtyard with her ducklings. The two mallard moms felt relieved and happy that their fears had been dispelled.

Blossom and Petals agreed that they would get together for a play date at the river after the next full moon. By then, Petals' young ducks would be able to fly with some confidence and unlike when they were first born, the two groups would not have any appreciable size difference. Together, they represented a sizable flock of mallards, which held much promise for the future.

Chapter 52
Third Grade

Dissection of a squid! Oh, my goodness. Helen had expected this third-grade field trip to the aquarium to be nice and simple, just shepherd students and chaperones through the exhibits. Now she had just learned that today's tour included an activity where each student was to cut apart a slimy tentacled creature from the ocean's depths and extract the ink sack it used to create a colored cloud in the water to escape from predators. They then would use the sack's ink to write their names on paper. She had not prepared her students for this challenge nor their parent chaperones, not to mention herself. She shuddered just thinking how it must smell and feel.

So far, her adventure in teaching third grade with its litany of standardized tests, added math and science curriculum, and cursive writing had been a non-stop march of just in time learning. She was now spending every night going over the next day's lesson generally for the first time. Black Friday during the Thanksgiving break she spent not in checkout lines at the mall but rather looking ahead over the lessons for the next six school days. Ironically, this was made possible by the computer linked to her smartboard which she now appreciated instead of loathed. Finally it reduced her work instead of doubling it. Her third-grade cohort Jean, a generous and gifted teacher, gave Helen all her prepared lessons on a little thumb drive. Helen now had very professional presentations without having to put in the copious hours of lesson development and production of presentation materials herself. All she had to do was plug in the thumb drive, and by the miracle of technology, look up the lesson file, open it, and present the material. *God, thank you for Jean*, she had prayed to the Almighty every time she opened another lesson.

The biggest new challenge to date had been the program of rotating science experiments done only last week. The third-grade teachers were each assigned a hands-on science experiment for which they developed the materials and process for students to perform. Each class of students would rotate through the teacher's classroom to do that teacher's experiment. Since this was a pilot program, teachers from the other elementary schools in the district were invited to observe. This resulted in her having over one-hundred student lab sheets of her experiment lesson plus comments from eight of her peers from other schools.

To her relief and frankly surprise, students and teachers seemed to enjoy her exercise on buoyancy. The experiment started by giving everyone the same amount of modeling clay. Each student first dropped the clay into a vat of water to witness that it sank. They then were asked to take the clay lump and form it into a boat. The boats were then placed on the water and loaded with pennies one at a time to see how many coins the boats could hold before they sank. The kids and teachers loved it.

"Please break up your class into teams of three," instructed the museum docent, "and have them gather around one of the dissection trays on the table where you will find your squids." The request brought Helen back to the present. With the odd number for each group, she ensured there was at least one girl or boy in each group, not knowing which gender might be the most squeamish. She then asked each parent to look over two teams of students.

When the teams got to their trays any assumption that boys would be more tolerant of the task ahead got blown away when Henry yelled, "There is no freaking way I am going to touch that. It's looking at me." It was clear that by their expression others were thinking the same thing, including some of the parents, and she too.

As Helen walked by, Lisa turned and tugged on her sleeve, and in a timid voice said, "Mrs. Dean, I really don't want to do this. It's icky." "Yes, Lisa, it is sort of icky. How about if you do it, I will do it too?" Helen replied to the sweet troubled little face. "OK, I'll try," said Lisa, and she immediately slashed into the bulbous head of her squid." Helen almost gagged when she saw the splayed open creature.

Chapter 53
Super Duck

The early December weather was about to change. The flock sensed it needed to move on from the New York coast toward the Barnegat refuge. As they resumed their migratory trip in the evening twilight, the south wind which had been blowing steady all day lost its momentum. The remaining daylight was eclipsed by a heavy wall of clouds approaching from the northwest. The barometric pressure dropped, allowing the air's moisture and pollutants to form a smoky fog over the coastline. Shying away from the fog bank, the flock flew inland, where the world below them turned into a web of light going to the horizon. Their familiar landmarks were lost in disorienting light patterns.

As the flock pressed forward, they found the wall of clouds to be advancing quickly. Calmness was replaced by a strong cross wind, which raked through the flock's flying formation of diagonal lines, driving them off course and farther inland over the web of lights. They then saw a large dark open area amid the ground lights. Thinking this might be an area of open water, the flock moved toward the open space by flying at an angle to the wind's direction, so they did not have to fight the wind's full force head on. They hoped they would find open water there and a familiar landmark in the process.

The clouds began moving faster and lowering, and the ground light was reflecting off the bottoms of them. The air now glowed between the clouds and the ground. In that strange yellow and pink light, she noticed super ducks descending and landing on the dark open grass, and then waddling down the length of the field. *This is where the super ducks* go, Blossom concluded. No sooner had she recognized this fact, there was a series of bright air-to-ground flashes of lightning, blinding and further disorienting the flock. A frigid hard burst of wind drove the flock back and sideways to their line of travel.

The pilot of United Flight 406 was on his final approach to Newark International runway 10 North, recognizing that he needed to get on the deck before the storm out his left window hit. Winds, however, are not always seen and despite the latest technology for detecting them, he found his Airbus 378 being tilted to the left as the 55-mph cross wind first caught the starboard front of the plane, and then lifted the starboard side wing. Continuing his descent now would be certain disaster for the plane and passengers, not to mention the facilities and people on the ground. His ground proximity warning started screaming, and his training kicked in as he and his first officer aborted the landing and fought to regain control of the aircraft, applying full power to its two Rolls-Royce engines to regain altitude and clear the field structures.

Blossom and the flock now were being accelerated upwards by the updraft caused by the arriving storm. As they rose, a set of bright lights came racing at them, and a super duck sliced through the flock. Blossom recoiled in disbelief as she slid over one of the super duck's wings, spinning in the turbulence of its slip stream's wake. She found herself tumbling uncontrolled in the air, losing sense of position and direction of travel. Up, down, sideways, it all was a mind overwhelming blur. Terrified, and with the induced vertigo caused by the storm cloud and mist, she finally realized she was inverted and falling as the air was pushing down on top of her wings. Tucking her wings so that her body rotated, she then felt herself moving forward with the now colder air filling her wings again and providing lift.

Uncertain still as to where she really was and wondering where the other members of the flock were, she stopped flapping and cupped her wings to begin a controlled glide into the wind. The storm moved past quickly, pushing the low clouds and fog ahead of it. Blossom finally started to see the glowing landscape below her. The storm's updraft had lifted her over 15,000 feet, and the view was unbelievable as she continued her slow descent and searched the surrounding air for the other members of her flock. Still in shock from the close encounter with the super duck, Blossom finally recognized a place that appeared to have plenty of open water. She continued a controlled descent to where she hoped to land and regroup her emotions. She needed to figure out what she would do next and how to find and rejoin the survivors of the super duck encounter.

Chapter 54
Peace

Helen's restored feeling of control in fact produced some different behaviors. On a Thursday night in mid-December, she heard on her husband's favorite television network, The Weather Channel, that the best time to see the Geminid Meteor Shower would be at two a.m. that night. Now there were two things that really fascinated Helen: oceans and stars. To her husband's surprise, Helen set their alarm clock to go off at one-thirty a.m. Knowing how tired she came home each day, he was baffled as to why she would want to get up at that time of night on a school night. They went to sleep, and when the alarm went off at one-thirty, Helen got out of bed and wrapped up in her gown and robe. She went into the front yard to peer up into the heavens. James was not so sure that this was such a great idea, as anytime he woke up at that time of night, he had a hard time going back to sleep. As he lay awake, he wondered what Helen was up to. Throwing on a pair of jeans, he trudged out and joined her. Indeed, there were meteors streaking across the moonless heavens.

After seeing ten or more meteors her husband retreated to the house, since Helen told him she wanted to stay out longer. Looking at the stars always made her feel small, but the magnificence of the night sky with its openness gave her some sort of release. It felt as if all her cares were being absorbed into the infinite expanse and its stars strewn through the darkness.

A minute later, James returned with an old sleeping bag, saying he thought Helen might enjoy not having to put a crick in her neck as she looked up. He spread it out on the front yard, laying a plastic poncho under it to block out the ground's moisture. James stepped into the open bag and said, "My lady, would you care to join me?" He laid down on the bag and held up his arm for her to join him, which she did. Then James pulled over the top half of the bag, and they snuggled together in the flannel-lined envelope on their backs while looking straight up at the galaxy and beyond. It was a refreshing experience spotting shooting stars, sometimes seeing the same one, and other times, missing one that the other saw. At about three in the morning, the number of shooting stars waned, and they returned to bed and slept soundly.

Chapter 55
New Reality

The peace and sense of awe engendered by the beautiful December night's sparkling beauty with its crescendos of streaking light were now gone. Her overloaded mind, unknown to her, now suppressed many of the horrific memories of the school day that have followed that glorious night. The magnitude and emotional those images wielded had to be put out of her consciousness so she could carry on and help herself, students, families, and colleagues. She knew things were bad, but when her husband told her the full extent of the situation, she knew her world and that for many others had changed forever.

Marble Brook Elementary School was closed for now. All the outpouring of emotion, the president's visit, the discussions about returning to teach the week after it occurred, then the postponement of classes until the new year seemed to be in a whole different world, place, time. Why God? Why? Why? The answer never came.

The question now was where and when classes would resume, at Marble Brook or dispersed to other elementary schools. Neither alternative sounded good for many reasons. Could they really go back to the old building after what had happened? Scattering children and families across other schools to environments where no one understood the emotions and challenges so many faced just seemed like adding insult to injury and even more disruption to all the young lives.

There was a rumor posted on Facebook that officials were considering moving the school to an empty junior high school in a neighboring town. Nice idea, but it was highly unlikely that an old junior high school could be configured to accommodate a K-4 elementary school. For now, it was encouraging to have the hope that Marble Brook Elementary School staff and students could remain together. She just wished she could wake up and find that it all had been a nightmare. Helen missed her students, so she decided to host a class gathering at the old town hall to help reassure them in some way that life would go on.

Chapter 56
Mild Winter

Their winter experience along the upper Atlantic coast was different than the recent past, as the coldest weather occurred in late December with a heavy snowfall; but the rest of the winter, the snowfalls were minimal; and by early March, some early blooming bulbs, like crocuses, could be seen popping their heads out of the ground. Optimism was high for an early spring, but every honest and experienced New Englander knew its weather never failed to disappoint. And sure enough, it did disappoint, as the bright sunny days of spring appeared to have been outlawed by Mother Nature through most of April into May. They were supplanted by a cloudy malaise of coolish weather with little character other than a gloomy sameness mixed with drizzle.

With the milder winter, Blossom and Petals, with their offspring, stayed farther north than in the recent past, hanging around the coastal farmland and rivers of Maryland and Northern Virginia. For a while, they stayed behind a building with tables situated along the back of its parking lot that abutted a nice deep pool of a slow flowing stream. Two leggers shared their food with them and in some cases, literally fed them out of their featherless appendages. The oiliness of some of the food did make it hard on their duck digestion though. Fortunately, they realized their mistake after a few days and moved on to healthier fields and food before their duck livers were permanently clogged.

Both Blossom and Petals had successfully found new mates in December along the Eastern shore of Maryland, but Petals had almost lost hers when they had decided to land in a cornfield. The smoking sticks had jumped from the ground, striking her mate with pellets, one raking a crease across the side of his head, leaving a permanent ripple in his dark green head feathers. Thankfully, none of the impacts were lethal or life threatening.

Chapter 57
Make it Happen

The decision was controversial, but it had been made. They would not be going back to the Marble Brook Elementary School building. It would be demolished in the hopes of erasing a trigger for the painful memories it now spawned.

The early rumor about converting a junior high school in a nearby town had become a reality. Credit the town officials for being decisive. Helen felt this was good news for the Marble Brook School staff, students, and families. The bad news was they had been given just two weeks to move into a new but temporary home. This only compounded what had been a challenging year for Helen as she tried to keep up with learning the third-grade curriculum. Now she was playing catch up on the physical classroom too.

All the desks, chairs, materials, books, rugs, projection equipment, and other resources had to be packed, labeled, transported, sorted, and set-up in the new space. The Christmas and New Year's school holiday break for the school administrators, teachers, and especially custodians had been a string of frantic ten-to-fourteen-hour days.

They had felt the love and compassion of so many outside of their school community as teachers from other town schools, a retired superintendent, principal, other administrators, including many from the host town schools, and personal friends had risen up to help them meet the challenge. Their custodial staff and school district employees lovingly worked themselves ragged to not disappoint and ensure the old junior high building was kindergarten through grade four functional when classes resumed in January, even though it might only be used till the end of the current school year.

The first day back in the converted junior high school, they had a mandatory evacuation drill which had gone better than feared, as the last time they had done an evacuation at the old school it had been for real. Children were thankfully resilient, and there had been little anxiety apparent as they left and returned from the evacuation assembly areas outside the temporary school building. Still standing in the cold, Helen could not help but feel a sense of vulnerability in being outside in the open, as she knew the office staff was having to field an unconscionable number of threats from teen pranksters and adults who felt the school was part of some left-wing political ruse. The burden on their minds and spirit was taking a toll.

The constant presence of the host town's police officers was providing a positive influence and a feeling of safety and protection that sadly was needed. The officers also added some comic relief, handing out little rubber duckies to the students in memory of the ducklings they had been told resided in the courtyard of the old school. Each rubber duck was dressed like some character or profession: a fisherman, policeman, pilot, dinosaur, Irishman, leprechaun, and one with a green ribbon on its white breast.

Despite their resilience, the students still picked up on the concern of their family and others for them while at school. The school nurse noted that visits to her were at a higher frequency than she had been seeing at the old school. One group that helped to reduce the anxiety and sadness was the Lutheran comfort dogs and their kind dedicated handlers. They had appeared soon after the temporary school facility opened. The golden retrievers were trained to be puddles of acceptance and love. Having a capacity to tolerate endless pats and hugs from all who approached; listening with kind eyes; being a quiet, non-threatening, and calming presence. Helen ensured that one of the four legged angels visited her classroom each day to provide moments of peace and true to their title, comfort to she and her students.

Chapter 58
Expectations

Despite the mild weather, they waited until the snow geese, then the brants and Canada geese had passed by before they started their own return north. Blossom and Petals both realized that the Marble Brook School nesting area had been a smashing success, but with that came other problems and added risks in rearing their young once they were successfully hatched. Both had confidence knowing they had the two leggers there to help and that they understood their needs. And despite the new challenges, they had still succeeded in a big way.

By the third day back in the Marble Brook courtyard, Blossom knew for sure something was different. The rumblers were missing from the white striped, black area next to the school. The doors and windows stayed shut. There were no speakers squawking, no chatter or laughter to be heard; the bird feeders were empty, no suet blocks either; the grass was not even; weeds were standing high above the grass; no golden feathered two legger and little ones looking out the windows by the holly bush; and the shrubs were splayed with new drooping, untrimmed growth. At night, the windows remained dark, and the two legger with the noise maker never made its rounds room to room. The stillness was conspicuous, with no vapor rising in the cool night air from the pipes on the roof. It appeared the two leggers, like a colony of bees, had left their old tree and swarmed to another home, a better place one would assume. The one thing that was unchanged was the apple tree, which had bright new blossoms bursting with the hope that only spring brings.

They reasoned that without the two leggers, Marble Brook was no longer the paradise it once had been. No little two leggers filling the feeders and water pan; no defenders against the hawks, no big two leggers to open the way for them to escape the courtyard and the raptors that tried to capture their ducklings. Blossom looked at Petals with sad eyes. Petals had shared with Blossom how tough things had been for her ducklings once Blossom had left, and about how she had talked to the two legger with the golden head feathers about needing more seed. But neither of them had seen or heard the golden headed two legger since they had returned.

They both knew this had been a special place, and they would miss their two-legger friends. They wished they could have at least said goodbye. Here, they both could share their continued love and companionship with their nests near each other. They would miss that feeling and assurance of having a loved one nearby. The world outside the courtyard would probably not allow it, and it had only been possible here because of the two leggers, whom Blossom had feared before she and Petals had experienced their help. Both mallard moms had gotten to know those special creatures. What a difference their friendship with the two leggers had made in both of their lives, allowing them to protect and hatch all the eggs they laid. "Where were they now?" they asked each other. "Why did they leave? Do they miss us?" It would be a mystery they would never understand or solve.

After the two mallards talked it over, Blossom encouraged Petals to go ahead and nest at the beaver pond, where she already understood the threats and challenges. Blossom would head to the lake backwater area, as last season she had spotted several areas that she thought might be good nesting sites. An especially promising one was where some two leggers had been putting out seed next to their boat dock. That boat dock, as well as several others along the same shoreline, could be good refuges from overhead threats. These structures attracted minnows and small fish to their cover and shade and would be high protein additions to their diet. If she found some good nesting areas, perhaps Petals could join her the following year at the lake. Hope was a wonderful thing not to lose, and especially useful when combined with courage.

Chapter 59
The Lake

Michael was on the dock when he saw a lone brown duck approaching, flying low, and then bank sharply and drop down in the middle of the lake channel off his dock. It had an orange beak and reminded him of the mother duck that had come into their yard the prior spring with her thirteen ducklings; maybe she was coming back. He dropped his fishing pole and headed to the garage to find the leftover birdseed and a little bucket, which he filled.

When he got back to the dock, he saw that the duck had moved up the lake to their neighbor's property, where it appeared to be investigating the shoreline and lake bank. He started spreading the seed along the grass embankment next to the lake. Picking up his fishing rod, he returned the seed pail to the garage and stowed his pole, then headed to the back deck to see if the duck would come to their yard. He had been waiting for a few minutes, when he heard his mom call him to do his homework. He took one last look at the shoreline to see if the duck had appeared before going inside. No luck, no duck.

He was working on his math at the dining room table, when his mom announced, "Michael, it looks like our mother duck may be back." "Where?" he asked. "She is out by the boat dock where you left seed last year." "Great! She found it," he replied. "She found what?" his mom queried. "The seed I just put out there. I saw her land in the middle of the channel and thought she might be our mother duck." "Well, whether she is or not, it appears she has found your seed." His mom smiled and nodded toward the dining room, pointing him back to his homework. Michael took a quick peek out the back window, and then turned his eyes back to his paper.

Blossom liked the forty-foot sided triangle of undisturbed growth between the two lawns. There were had some low bushes and taller saplings that comprised a thicket, sitting on top of the bank next to the lake. As she recalled, there had not been any dogs or other creatures seen on the side of the property where the two leggers with the birdseed lived. On the other side was the yappy dog, which sounded threatening but never attacked. Unlike the beaver pond, the lakeside properties for the most part were devoid of old growth trees but had mostly open lawn with a few small shrubs.

With such a barren landscape, this potential nesting site did not have the predator pressure that surrounded the beaver pond. The nearest woods were across the lake channel, but on this side, the forest was almost a half mile away; reachable but not convenient for marauding raccoons, half blind skunks, foxes, bobcats, and the like, although that was not to say that they and coyotes might not run through the neighborhood at times. The lack of deep field grass limited the proximity to rat snakes, and the dirt and small gravel shoreline did not provide the cover preferred by the common water snakes. Swans and Canada geese were much more likely to visit than one of the furry or scaly marauders.

There was one major difference; a new type of rumbler that went splashing by on the lake. They had all sorts of things following behind them, including two leggers standing up and sliding back and forth behind them, kicking up sprays of water. Often when these new rumblers went by in the lake channel, a large series of waves would suddenly appear and beat against the shore, turning the shallow water into a cloudy slurry of silt, algae, and water plants. This made snacking a lot easier without having to do a head down, tail up search of the lake bottom.

Blossom decided to stay and see what happened there during the dark hours. As the light faded over the hill located behind all the houses, the clearing moonless sky came alive with stars, and the water stilled to an inky smoothness. She heard a group of geese landing down the lake, making noise as they greeted others who were already there to rest for the night. Across the lake channel she could see the lights and hear a land rumbler, vibrating along the road that came from the dam site. It moved along the far lake shore to where it met another highway before going over a steel truss bridge that spanned the lake's old narrow river channel.

From time to time, she heard far away two legger voices and a passing rumbler on one of the residential streets of the neighborhood, but as the night progressed, the only sounds were owls and peepers looking for mates accompanied by a soft low tone of a wind chime when the wind stirred softly. Blossom still kept one eye open, but the night proved wonderfully uneventful. The sun rose with a lot of promise for a new nesting experience.

The following week, she paddled around the general area, but Blossom deliberately stayed away from the lakeside thicket during the day. Only in the late evening and early morning did she go to inspect and add to her growing clutch of eggs, which she had covered with a mixture of down, feathers, grass, and leaves until she began their incubation.

She did note that the two leggers were coming and going from the boat dock more often and that a small water rumbler was now tied to it. She was always a little nervous when she heard it start making noise and bubble its way into the lake with one to three two leggers in it. Odd, but not uncommon, as she had grown accustomed to seeing more rumblers pass by. Strangely, the water rumblers and their appendages would be very active for two days, but most times, only two or three appeared. She observed that when it was sunny and warm with little or no wind, the rumblers were more active, and every few days a smallish two legger came and poured seed on the bank, next to the dock, where she and her ducklings had eaten last season. As at Marble Brook, she went to collect it in the late evenings and early mornings, when two legger and rumbler activity was low.

After she added the thirteenth egg to the clutch, Blossom went on a one-day eating binge, risking some added exposure to ensure she had plenty of nourishment before she was restricted to keeping the eggs warm. Things were going well so far, and she hoped that Petals was also having good luck at the beaver pond. The white-headed eagles were sailing over, but they consistently glided past, not stopping. They rested in the trees lining the opposite side of the lake, apparently keeping their distance from any encounter with the two leggers on her side, which was fine with her.

There also was another large, mostly white raptor with a black stripe across it eyes, which seemed to track the schools of shad that would periodically boil up to the surface. These different raptors would hover in one spot high above the fish, and then quickly dive into the pod legs first, momentarily floating on the surface, their elongated forewings raised like one of the small seagulls that also inhabited the lake. With its wings elevated high above the water and its captured silvery meal in its talons, this raptor's wings easily lifted it up off the water, and then it flew to its favorite perch up on a high tree limb to enjoy its fresh catch.

Blossom had noticed that the eagles seemed to be attacked by all sorts of other birds and were especially pestered by crows, which she did not especially like either. One day, there appeared to be a turf war between an eagle and one of the white raptors, who had a sizable fish dangling off one leg that the eagle apparently wanted. The eagle quickly descended and rammed into the other white raptor mid-air, knocking it sideways and causing it to lose its fish, which tumbled down and splatted stunned and motionless on the lake's surface. The eagle then brushed off its opponent, circled down to the water, and snatched up the fish deftly, and then with a triumphant screech headed toward the dam, no doubt to feed its eaglets.

Chapter 60
Tornado

The school district had an exceptional number of snow days that year, so state law required that the last day of the year be extended to June sixteenth. Helen and her family had planned to fly to Oklahoma to visit relatives the weekend following the last day of school, a Thursday. Then, as luck would have it, a powerful thunderstorm spawned a tornado that came within two-tenths of a mile from their home. Ironic, in that her husband had grown up near eastern Oklahoma, part of "tornado alley," and had never missed a school day there because of a tornado. Now, living in quiet New England, the weather gods decide to wreak havoc this spring of all springs where they lived.

They did not actually experience the storm, for they had traveled to Maryland for their daughter's graduation from medical school but then had immediately left after dinner to drive home. They had expected to get back well after midnight. As they got closer to home, they noticed tree limbs and small logs cut up alongside the state highway that ran a half mile from their house. At first, they thought it must have been power utility tree crews who had been working to cut back trees from the electrical lines, as there had been a rash of ice and wind events that knocked out power over the past year.

As they progressed further, the size of the tree debris kept increasing, with large tree trunks cut up along the road. Rounding the sweeping ninety-degree curve of the state highway that headed to their turnoff, they saw a line of power poles laying sideways away from the road and dozens of trees laid down in the same direction. This blowdown occurred when their roots were pulled up out of the ground.

None of the houses had any lights on. Streetlights were out. When they arrived at their own home, the garage door openers did not work. Fortunately, there did not appear to be any damage to their house and the seventy-foot oaks had held tight to their rocky ledges and did not fall. They learned later that they were very fortunate to have experienced unobstructed roads to their house.

The F-1 twister had traveled on the ground across the town from west to east, knocking out power and blocking roads. Hundred-year-old trees were toppled across its six-mile path. One towering red oak had guillotined a neighbor's house. The tree went through the upper floor family room picture window and the sliders off the dining room and onto the back deck before being stopped by the concrete foundation. Fortunately, there were no deaths or serious injuries, but this storm's damage resulted in schools being canceled for two days as utility and town crews worked to reopen all the bus routes. These cancelations moved the end of school from a Thursday to the following Monday. Delaying the last day of school by four days meant they were having to cancel their original reservations and pay change fees and higher air fares for the trip to see parents and family.

Chapter 61
Injured

Michael's new morning routine was to first slip on his shorts and sneakers and fill a can of seed to feed the duck who was hanging around their dock. Today he was doing it sooner because he needed to be at school early to meet up with some classmates to work on a skit, they were to do in their first period history class.

As he poured out the seed, he was startled to see the mallard hen appear abruptly from under the dock making lots of noise. It was flapping like it was trying to take off but kept crashing back into the water, flying briefly, and crashing again and again down the shoreline. He dumped out the rest of the seed and went in pursuit. *Was she injured?* he wondered. *Perhaps she had a broken wing. Had she gotten tangled into some fishing line carelessly discarded or broken off by some fisherman?* Every time he got close, it squawked and struggled to fly farther down the shoreline. Despite the injury, it still managed to stay just out of reach. He gave up realizing he still needed to eat breakfast and get ready for school. He would have to check in on it later.

Coming into the kitchen his mom greeted him with "Good

morning. How's my man this morning? Did you sleep well? Here's your waffle and bacon," handing him the plate along with a glass of orange juice. "Thanks Mom" he responded, taking the food, and sitting down at the counter.

"Are things alright?" his mother asked, having noted he had not answered her questions and he obviously had something on his mind.

"I was down at the dock putting out the seed and I saw the mallard hen and she looked like she was injured."

"How so?" his mom inquired.

"She was squawking, flapping her wings but seemed unable to fly away. She kept crashing back into the water," Michael shared with concern. "I am afraid she has a broken wing or has gotten wrapped up in some fishing line."

His mom smiled as she recalled a similar duck encounter when she was about Michael's age and visiting her Uncle Bob in Vermont. Her uncle had taken her to a remote pond on his property where there was a mother duck who had done the same thing Michael was describing. Like Michael, she thought the duck had broken a wing. Her uncle pointed out that the duck was not injured but she was faking injury in hopes of luring them away from her ducklings. He then pointed out a nest that was located just up the shoreline that had ducklings still in it.

"Did you see any ducklings?" his mom asked. "No, why?" he responded, looking up at her while biting into a piece of bacon. Her eyes brightened as she shared her own mother duck encounter. As she shared her memory, she knew the moment her son recognized what he had seen.

"I am going to look to see if there are any ducklings when I get home from ball practice. I hope you are right about there are ducklings" he declared and quickly finished the last of his orange juice. He then headed to brush his teeth and pack his school bag so his mom could take him to meet his classmates.

Michael's family enjoyed seeing the mother duck with a new

group of ducklings visiting their yard. They still did not realize that the ducklings had been incubated and hatched just over a hundred feet from their boat dock.

The summer's days marched by quickly, and the new ducklings grew fast, benefiting from the birdseed and the wide variety of high protein foods offered by the lake. Michael occasionally surprised them when he ran out to the dock to fish or leave seed. Several times he found them hiding under the dock's deck of weathered planks. Blossom would appear and lead her troop away but not with any of the lame duck theatrics she had employed when the little ones were just hatchlings. Now she just quacked at him and coaxed her flock to move away.

Chapter 62
Separate Worlds

Periodically, a pair of mute swans had come by with their cygnets. These large waterfowl were now a fixture on many lakes, having been imported for their beauty and inability to cackle and honk loudly. Owners introduced them to their private ponds and lakes; but as often is the case with invasive species, they eventually moved and bred outside those intended confines and the native waterfowl had to adjust to these large foreign invaders.

Blossom and her ducklings had been swimming near the back water where the river entered the lake, eating algae and water plants that thrived on the soft mud bottom, when the much larger waterfowl decided they wanted to dine there too. The parents, with their long necks extended, hissed their way into the little cove, clearly demanding that Blossom and the ducklings leave so that they and their cygnets could have it all for themselves. Blossom, outsized and outnumbered by the adult swans, moved her brood quickly back up the lake shore, not wanting a fight she knew would not be good for herself and her dependents. Ever since then,

Blossom kept her family at a safe distance from the prima donnas and their drab gray cygnets.

Meanwhile, Petals had found the experience at the beaver pond for the most part a repeat of the past. Chomps and Cuddles, the pond's senior citizens, still lurked mostly unseen, and two ducklings just disappeared. Of the thirteen eggs she had laid and started to incubate, only eleven had survived to hatch thanks the unwelcomed visit of the rat snake. The slithering reptile had one lump showing in its body and was just completing its ingestion of a second egg, when Petals had returned from a meal break. She pecked hard at the snake's tail, keeping away from its head. With its mouth full, the snake curled as if to strike but satisfied with what it had already swallowed, turned, and retreated without further challenge or theft.

Despite the rat snake incident, she had enjoyed much greater success than in her earlier experience at the pond. Her mad mother duck attitude had come out again when an unfamiliar great blue heron with bright golden eyes attempted to spear one duckling that had moved too far from Petals and near the tall motionless bird. Seeing the blue bully go after her baby had triggered her to react violently toward the much larger animal. Launching herself with a guttural "QUACK," she had hit big blue squarely in the neck, going for the jugular and thwarting the heron's ability to complete its duckling capture. It had all happened in less than two seconds, and Petals quacked an earful at the confused heron.

In late August, the first cool dry breezes of fall rippled the pond's surface, with a total of twenty-one fledged ducks now flying and roaming beyond their rearing areas. A few maple trees had leaves turning bright yellow-orange and reinforced the feeling that summer would end soon.

Although not the same number as they had been able to hatch at Marble Brook courtyard the prior season, both mothers felt fortunate to have again produced two wonderful groups of beautiful mallards on their own. Hopefully they would be seeing each other again soon, as they and their little flocks and other mallards joined the annual trip south for the period of short cold days.

Chapter 63
Done

Helen felt her new classroom was as ready as it was going to be. In some ways things were a lot simpler than at Marble Brook, since being located on a second floor and having the building surrounded by a parking lot, it was not practical or feasible to have any bird feeders. She missed the apple tree, the birds, and most of all the potential in the spring of seeing a mother duck with her ducklings. She hoped that the ducks did not find themselves trapped in the old courtyard. She put that sad thought out of her mind. The job list also had fewer tasks allowing her students to go outside the classroom. This was due in part to the more complex two-story building layout plus a desire to know at any moment the location of each student, as the event had proven that important.

Last year, she had found a route to and from the temporary school using the back country roads, which avoided using the state highways with their faster traffic and stop lights. Most days, the state road route would be the fastest way home, but that was not what she wanted or needed. Her husband seldom if ever came home early from his job, so there was no reason nor desire to rush home to an empty house. The roads she was taking wound through wooded stretches of residential homes, small farms, forest, and high meadows. She was now passing the little theater building where the local amateur thespians performed; the road then made a dog leg to cross the bridge over a brook that James said had native brook trout. Her route then continued up the hill under a canopy of oaks and through several residential street intersections, cresting in a high meadow with a panoramic view of tree covered hills that rolled slowly down to the coast.

Here old stone walls with intermittent trees lined the meadow lane. Over the wall on the right side, she saw the grass air strip where propeller driven, lightweight aircraft took off and landed. The hangar with its small control tower, an octagon of windows nestled on its roof, reminded her of World War II movies that showed army air corps installations in the English countryside. Today the long international orange windsock hung limp on its thirty-foot pole at the far end of the field, and she wondered just how much wind a pilot needed to safely clear the seventy-five-foot tree line hazard on either end of the mowed runway.

As she passed the small hangar, her attention was drawn to the opposite side of her windshield where some seventy plus year old 'kids' were flying their remote-controlled model airplanes. She had to do a quick course correction after she tried to catch sight of the miniature planes that were looping high above their owners' heads. The scene reminded her of her own dad, who after retirement, had built several model planes, and like these men, enjoyed the camaraderie created by sharing in the creation, testing, flying, crashing, and repairing their paper, balsa, and glue aerial babies.

She slowed for the stop sign, and then made her right turn on a section of sparsely populated road that was straight until it came to another crossroad stop sign. She waited as a lone SUV went by, and then proceeded on to a winding section of road that traveled through several small farms. Helen smiled as she saw a couple of horses standing motionless in the small corral next to their barn.

She had always wanted to take up riding again, like she was able to do when she was a teenager living at Quantico Marine Corps Base. She used to sit high in the air and was free to roam.

Making it through a pair of small bends and a short dip, she then saw her friends the burros, with their large eyes and long eyelashes, who for some strange reason always seemed to run toward the fence when she drove by. "Hello, Mr. and Mrs. Burro," she said, waving. Of course, the burros were probably thinking how strange it was that person in the car was waving and talking to them. He-haw, he-hawing and stamping their front hooves in reply. She chuckled at the thought.

Taking her foot off the gas and allowing the car to coast, she approached the curve in front of the old Apple Hill farmhouse and barn. The acreage had recently been acquired by the local land trust and other than the farm buildings and their two-acre plot, the rest of the property would be maintained as wild open space. At the three-way intersection by the street corner near the farmhouse, she turned and followed the narrow roadway along the land trust property. She now drove slowly, as the underbrush and tree cover were thick, and being adjacent to a large undeveloped area meant a deer could quickly appear and rearrange her car grill. Thankfully, today there no deer were struck, but she would not have minded seeing some.

She finally emerged from the tunnel of undergrowth to come to her favorite corner on the trip. It was not a large property at all; it had a strong wood fence perimeter around a corral and in the middle was a covered feed and hay trough. A decent sized barn was inserted into the fence-line on the side that faced the back of the owner's house. The attractive home faced a roadway in front that separated it from a forty-acre marshland.

What she loved about this place were the five highland cattle that resided in the corral. These massive, broad shouldered, short legged mounds of orange-brown hair with their eye covering bangs looked like something Jim Henson would have used as a pattern for a Muppet bovine character. They also reminded her of their trip to Scotland, the open countryside, and cattle as they had traveled between Glasgow, Isle of Skye, Balmoral Castle, Inverness, Edinburgh, and Saint Andrews. She smiled as she passed by the cattle and remembered a night in the inn outside Inverness, when trying to get to sleep. There was a wedding downstairs and at midnight the celebrants began singing "Loch Lomond" so the whole countryside could hear, "You take the high road, and I'll take the low road, and I'll be in Scotland before you, where me and my true love will never meet again, on the Bonnie, Bonnie banks of Loch Lomond."

As she finally approached her street, she hoped that she would be able to keep all the happy memories going before her true love got home from work. Just as she was wondering what to make for dinner, her phone buzzed, and she saw James' text: "Headed home, how about going to Pepe's for dinner, my treat." She thought, "Bonnie, bonnie good my true love; bonnie, bonnie good." This would leave her little time by herself when so often the bad memories rushed in and filled her spirit with darkness. She had enough time to freshen up so that she and James could enjoy a nice quiet dinner that she did not have to cook. "Bonnie, bonnie good."

Chapter 64
Lonely Summer

The summer break was void of any family vacations for Randy Jackson who would be in fourth grade the coming fall. He had spent two weeks with his Aunt Cheryl, though, who had offered to have him visit. She was very kind and had taken him to a minor league ball game and a science center. The science center had all sorts of exhibits on dinosaurs, various mechanical exhibits with weights and pulleys, and an interactive floor projector where he got to play games by stepping on different spots projected on the floor to score points. They had also gone to Boston and saw a big aquarium that had huge sharks and all sorts of other funny shaped and colorful fish, jellyfish, other sea creatures, and a sea lion show. He loved being with her and getting to eat his favorite things and some new things too that she cooked. Most of all, she always had a smile for him.

The rest of the summer during the day, he was pretty much on his own, as his older siblings played soccer and lacrosse several days a week and often slept over at friends' homes. His dad traveled a lot, and his mother worked in an office down near the coast, which meant she was gone all day until late afternoon. Most days he played some hand me down video games and watched programs on television, most often alone.

Today, the first day of school, he was up early and dressed so that his mom could take him to the bus stop as she headed out to work. He was wearing a pair of shorts and knit shirt he had pulled out of a clothes basket, as well as his brother's old Adidas sneakers without socks. His mom had given him a new spiral notebook and some unsharpened pencils that she had gotten at work.

The bus appeared, stopping on the opposite side of the road, deploying its side mounted stop sign, and extending a barrier on the front bumper. He looked both ways and saw that cars were stopped, and it was safe to proceed. He crossed, grabbed the railing, pulled himself up on the first step, and then on up the steps as the grey-haired bus driver named Bud said, "Welcome aboard a new school year. Good to see you back." Randy half looked up and gave an emotionless stare, then walked back to a seat in the middle of the bus, still looking down and avoiding any eye contact with others who were already on board. As he sat down, the bus began to move.

As was the case when school ended in the spring, his bus ride again would be to the temporary school in the next town. As they bounced along and made three more stops, his mind wondered how things would be this year. He did not know his teacher, Mrs. Miller, and he hoped that someone would tell him where her room was when he got there.

Eight minutes after the last student boarded, the bus pulled around the school's circular drive, stopping just past the front entrance. The driver set the brake and opened the front door, saying, "All ashore that are going ashore, front row first," and the students proceeded to file out, and Randy fell in line. When he stepped down on the asphalt he watched where the other students were headed, merging into the flow hesitantly.

As he stepped into the school, an adult volunteer asked, "Do you need help finding your room." "Ye-ye-yes" he choked out.

"Mrs. Miller." She flipped a page and said, "She is in room 280, which is on the second floor, up the steps to your right."

He moved down the upstairs hall, where students started disappearing into rooms. He finally came to room 280 and peeked in, fearing he would not know anyone. He saw a young, slender brunette escorting a boy to his desk. He froze for a moment, feeling a little overwhelmed. After the boy was seated, the woman looked around at him, standing in the doorway. "Welcome. I'm Mrs. Miller," she smiled waving him in. Since she was a new teacher and he had not met her, he hesitated. He avoided looking at her as he entered, staring at a waste basket. "And who do I have the pleasure of meeting this morning?" she inquired, tilting her head down to make eye contact with him. "I'm Randy Jackson," he said in a hoarse monotone. "Good to meet you, Randy. Let me show you where your desk and cubby are." He followed her to a set of free-standing cases with small compartments, each equipped with two coat hooks. His was marked by a colorful laminated label with his first name. "And over here is your desk," she said, leading him to a desk on the far side of the room that had another colorful personalized laminated label attached above the pencil rest.

As Mrs. Miller walked away, he heard a young soft voice behind him say his name. He turned around to see Danielle standing close behind him. *Danielle!* She instantly hugged him. It was a real hug, which conveyed sincerity and feeling. "Thank you," Danielle said, "for protecting me," then she hugged him again.

He could not help but think about the one-hundred-day celebration in second grade. His answer to "What would you want a hundred of?" would now be, "Mrs. Dean, I want a hundred of these hugs from Danielle." This was the best feeling ever! He smiled.

Epilogue

etals and Blossom were watching their two groups of nine and eleven ducklings respectively, splashing, spinning, and diving in the shoreline shallows next to the boat dock platform. It had been a remarkable spring, and the mystery of Marble Brook still bobbed around in their memories and thoughts.

When first arriving back, Blossom had visited the beaver pond, as was her habit, just in case the two leggers had returned and decided to drop in on the Marble Brook courtyard. What she found was very disorienting; hard to accept and absorb at first. Marble Brook had vanished. *When did it leave, and how? Where did it go?* she puzzled. She had circled the area several times and finally, when reoriented, she recognized the ball fields. She was sure it was the spot, but the building and courtyard were gone, without a trace. The two leggers would not be returning because there was no Marble Brook school to return to.

The mallard moms fondly recalled how the Marble Brook two leggers had helped them. Though not the same, a two-legger relationship had also developed at the lake in a very different but still positive way. The two leggers' water and land rumblers, coupled with the location of their homes, had posed an uncertain threat, but on the other forewing, they still provided food and a certain protection by keeping other predators at a distance. The ducks' understanding and attitude toward them were now different, as they had learned to adapt to different environments occupied by two leggers. They had become more like the Canada geese they saw in odd locations around buildings and roadway exchanges, resting and foraging on patches of grass located nowhere near any water. In fact, it seemed like the large black and white waterfowl were more plentiful than ever before. They would be wise to learn from their goose brethren and start looking for the opportunities to leverage available resources and not spend so much time in a xenophobic state of mind, avoiding and fearing the unknown.

Raptors they understood, and they were still a big concern in the spring when they like the ducks were trying to raise and feed their young. The craziest circus occurred in the fall when the young newly fledged raptors started to establish their own hunting territories that infringed on older and more experienced birds. It was that time of year when the raptors were most unpredictable because the young ones were still on a learning curve that involved some experimentation that at times seemed crazy and reckless, but it was simply just young adults engaged in their learning process, who were producing some odd, unpredictable behaviors, with sometimes tragic consequences. That was one of the benefits of being part of a flock. It was important and smart to learn from one's own mistakes, but it was wiser to listen and learn from other's mistakes, as one's odds for survival were greatly improved.

One thing both mallards were sure of, to survive they must continue to adapt and learn to deal with changes in the two-legger world around them. As they watched their ducklings and quietly talked about the struggles and success that they had both experienced, they felt the sunlight dim. A shadow appeared on the water, and both mallards blurted out, "Quack!! Qua-qua-a-ack!!!!" and twenty ducklings all dove instantaneously, leaving two clusters of expanding, interlocking rings on the water's surface.

The End.

Afterword

Wildlife and humans impact each other every day. Fear on both sides of the relationship, lack of knowledge of the other, ignorance concerning mutual dependency, plus conflicts of perceived and real needs cripple efforts for understanding and respect. Left on its own, the natural world works toward a balance or equilibrium. Nature's interactions may seem violent and often gross to our current human senses, but they are a necessary relationship that sustains the collective health of the many complex eco-systems.

Screen driven humans more than ever see nature as a threat to be eliminated or contained; vice versa nature's wildlife and other creatures see humans and their technology as overwhelming, merciless, and too often destructive and a threat to their survival both directly and indirectly. As we saw at Marble Brook, human activity impacts the natural world which if robust can absorb and adjust to restore its equilibrium of life.

Human capabilities and technologies too often interfere with the natural eco-systems. Out of fear, misconception of what is helpful, or just for our convenience, enjoyment, or comfort; we break food webs and the destroy tropic levels that are essential to a healthy sustainable natural world.

We the stewards of all life too often do not have the knowledge or technical capability to understand the consequences of our actions on nature and ultimately ourselves. We consume resources and destroy not only to sustain ourselves but too often to feed ego and pride, falsely boasting about our superiority and independence from nature and other humans. If we continue to exceed Nature's capacity to reproduce, recharge and handle our waste, we should not be surprised when our ecosystem in Nature no longer supports us.

Acknowledgments

Thanks first to my wife Robin for her inspiration, love, support, encouragement, and willingness to listen and guide me from a teacher's unique perspective. My appreciation to Stephanie and Desain Terry, along with Mary Harrington of Enterprise Studios, for their personal and professional assistance when I was struggling with how to proceed with this project.

My gratitude to C. D. (Doug) Peterson, a published author through traditional publishing houses, who encouraged me to write and publish, and whose wisdom helped me move past my doubts about producing this book, sharing that guidance while we traveled to and from fly fishing outings on local streams and lakes.

To my editor Rebecca Reid, who, beyond her guidance on writing and edits, provided objective insight into what was needed to help readers unfamiliar with the events that inspired the book to follow the storyline.

Acknowledgments

I am grateful too for Catherine St. Georges whose enthusiasm for nature and its wonders and experience as a teacher confirmed many concepts, provided helpful guidance and content that reduced undesired bias and judgement which would not have fulfilled my writing goal.

Thanks to my sister Becky for her love, support and for proofreading the manuscript so it was ready for production.

Finally, I would not have completed the project without the SPS team and my coach Barbara Hartzler, who with good humor and patience guided me through the process for producing and publishing this book.

Excerpt from "My Ballad of Robin Lee"

by James Randall

Excerpt from "My Ballad of Robin Lee"

ROBIN LEE, ROBIN LEE
THANKS FOR TEACHING ME
SELFLESS EFFORTS EACH DAY
NOT FOR GLORY, NOT FOR PAY
HELPING OTHERS IS WHAT YOU DO
AS YOUR LOVE COMES SHINING THROUGH
AS YOUR LOVE COMES SHINING THROUGH

ROBIN LEE, ROBIN LEE
THANKS FOR TOUCHING ME
HUMBLE IN SPIRIT, NOT DRIVEN BY PRIDE
YOU PROVIDE SAFE HARBOR FOR ME TO CONFIDE
YOU WEIGH WITH WISDOM WHAT TO SHARE
TOUCHING HEARTS AND MINDS EVERYWHERE
TOUCHING HEARTS AND MINDS EVERYWHERE

ROBIN LEE, ROBIN LEE
THANKS FOR SHARING WITH ME
THOSE COLLEAGUES WHO HELP YOU EACH DAY
THOSE LOVELY PEOPLE FOR WHOM YOU PRAY
HOW SPECIAL THEY ARE, GOOD AND TRUE
SPECIAL, SPECIAL PEOPLE JUST LIKE YOU
SPECIAL, SPECIAL PEOPLE JUST LIKE YOU

ROBIN LEE, ROBIN LEE CAN'T YOU SEE?
WITHOUT YOU I WOULD BE A LESSER ME
IN MY HEART YOU ALWAYS RESIDE
THANKS FOR SAYING YES AND BEING MY BRIDE
OVER FORTY YEARS MY PARTNER AND FRIEND
LORD MAY HER LOVE KNOW NO END
LORD MAY HER LOVE KNOW NO END